G000278640

DAYS IN THE LIFE

READING THE

MICHAEL COLLINS

DIARIES

1918–1922

BY

ANNE DOLAN AND WILLIAM MURPHY

An Chartlann Náisiúnta
National Archives

Acadamh Ríoga na hÉireann
Royal Irish Academy

Days in the life: reading the Michael Collins diaries, 1918–1922

First published 2022
Royal Irish Academy, 19 Dawson Street, Dublin 2
www.ria.ie

Published in partnership with the National Archives, Ireland.
www.nationalarchives.ie

ISBN 978-1-80205-003-5 (HB)

ISBN 978-1-80205-004-2 (pdf)

ISBN 978-1-80205-005-9 (epub)

British Library Cataloguing in Publication Data. A CIP catalogue record for this book is available from the British Library.

Designed by New Graphic
Proofread by Liz Evers
Printed in Italy by Printer Trento
Printed on Munken Lynx Rough annd Munken White 120gsm and 300gsm which is FSC-C020637, PEFC™ PEFC/05-33-99 certified.

Royal Irish Academy is a member of Publishing Ireland, the Irish book publishers' association

5 4 3 2 1

We want to try to offset the environmental impacts of carbon produced during the production of our books and journals. This year we will plant 45 trees with Easy Treesie (Crann Project, CHY13698).

Published with support from the Department of Tourism, Culture, Arts, Gaeltacht, Sport and Media under the Decade of Centenaries 2012–2023 Programme.

**An Roinn Turasóireachta, Cultúir
Ealaíon, Gaeltachta, Spóirt agus Meán**
Department of Tourism, Culture,
Arts, Gaeltacht, Sport and Media

CONTENTS

FOREWORD

In November 2021, the Michael Collins Diaries 1918–1922, were officially loaned to the National Archives by the family of the late Liam Collins, a nephew of Michael Collins, and his wife Betty, of Clonakilty, County Cork. The handover of the diaries took place at Woodfield near Clonakilty, the ancestral home of Michael Collins, a place he loved and returned to throughout his short life.

This deposit, in the context of the State's Decade of Centenaries 1912–1923 Commemorations Programme, was hugely significant for the National Archives. It not only recognised the statutory role of the National Archives in preserving and protecting the memory of the State in the form of its written records but it also recognised the substantial contribution made by Michael Collins to the emergence of the Irish Free State from 1916 to his death in 1922.

One of our most historical collections are the early Dáil Éireann papers which offer important insight into Ireland's revolutionary period 1918–1923. Amongst these records are those of the then Minister of Finance, Michael Collins. These papers, from formal correspondence, internal memos, hastily written notes, receipts and accounts, demonstrate a man not only committed to his country and its pursuit of independence but also an exacting, precise and decisive man conscious of the huge responsibility he carried in his many positions, from Chairman of the Irish Provisional Government to Commander in Chief of the National Army.

We were delighted therefore that the Collins family deposited these important diaries in the National Archives. We were equally delighted when Anne Dolan and William Murphy, biographers of Michael Collins, agreed to come on board as authors of a book that would explore and respond to the diaries in the overall context of the life of Michael Collins.

The authors do not seek to offer answers or unlock previous mysteries, rather they gently walk us through recurring themes, moments, people, found in the diary entries, opening up possibilities, making connections or offering interpretations based on their knowledge and insight into the man and this period in our history.

This book, based on new primary source material and coming in the year of the centenary of the death of Michael Collins in August 1922, has been a labour of love for many; those of us in the National Archives, the authors, William and Anne, and the Collins family. We hope that it will allow people to understand a little more of this extraordinary man and this complex period in the life of the nation.

Orlaith McBride
Director, National Archives

TIMELINE

1890	16 October	Collins born at Woodfield, Clonakilty, County Cork
1906	Summer	Moved to London to work for the Post Office Savings Bank
1908 c.		Joined Sinn Féin
1909	July	Became secretary of the Geraldines GAA Club
	November	Joined the Irish Republican Brotherhood (IRB)
1914	January (c.)	Irish Volunteers founded in London and Collins joined
1916	January (c.)	Military Services Act passed and Collins moved to Dublin
1916	24 April	Joined the Easter Rising, based at GPO
	May	Deported and interned at Stafford and then Frongoch Camp
	December	Released from Frongoch Camp
1917	14 February	Appointed paid secretary of the Irish National Aid & Volunteer Dependents' Fund (INA&VDF)
	June	Became a member of the Supreme Council of the IRB
	25 September	Thomas Ashe died on hunger strike: Collins became secretary of the Supreme Council of the IRB
	25–26 October	Sinn Féin Árd Fheis, Collins elected to the Executive
	27 October	Became director of organisation of the Irish Volunteers
1918	March	Became adjutant general of Irish Volunteers
	2 April	Arrested at Dublin, relating to a speech at Legga, Co. Longford
	20 April	Instructed while in Sligo Gaol to give bail

1918	May	Became a member of Sinn Féin Standing Committee (SFSC)
	6 July	Ceased to be secretary of INA&VDF
	19 September	SFSC confirmed Collins as candidate for South Cork
	December	Returned for South Cork unopposed at General Election
1919	21 January	Dáil Éireann met for the first time
	22 January	Became minister of home affairs, Dáil cabinet
	3 February	Participated in rescue of Éamon de Valera from Lincoln prison
	2 April	Collins appointed secretary for finance, Dáil cabinet
	May/June	Harry Boland and de Valera departed for USA
	May (c.)	Collins replaced Boland as president of the IRB
	mid-year	Appointed director of intelligence of Irish Volunteers
	30 July	Shootings of DMP officers by 'The Squad' began
	September	Dáil loan launched
1920	9 August	Restoration of Order in Ireland Act
	September	Dáil loan closed
	21 November	Bloody Sunday
	23 December	Government of Ireland Act became law; de Valera returned to Dublin
1921	13 May	Elected to southern parliament unopposed for Cork
	24 May	Elected to northern parliament for South Armagh
	11 July	The truce came into force
	14 September	Appointed a plenipotentiary to Anglo-Irish Conference
	6 December	Signed Anglo-Irish Agreement (The Treaty)
	19 December	Addressed Dáil Éireann, defending the Treaty

TIMELINE

1922	*c.*1 January	Collins and Kitty Kiernan became engaged
	7 January	Dáil Éireann approved the Treaty
	9 January	The anti-Treaty party withdrew from Dáil Éireann
	10 January	Appointed minister for finance (Dáil cabinet)
	14 January	Became chairman of the Provisional Government of the Irish Free State
	16 January	Took over Dublin Castle
	21 January	First Craig–Collins Pact signed
	March	Made a series of speeches defending the Treaty
	30 March	Second Craig–Collins Pact signed
	20 May	Signed pre-election pact with de Valera
	14 June	Collins made speech in Cork seen as breaking the pact
	16 June	Irish Free State Constitution published, General Election held, and Collins re-elected TD
	22 June	Sir Henry Wilson killed in London
	28 June	Civil War began
	5 July	Republican forces in Dublin surrendered and the fighting moved beyond the city
	12 July	Collins appointed 'Commander-in-Chief of the army' at head of three-man 'War Council'
	22 August	Collins killed at Béal na mBláth, County Cork

READING THE MICHAEL COLLINS DIARIES

The pages are not blank. In his diaries, Michael Collins chose to write particular words, on particular days. Usually, though not always, the words are identifiable. That has not ensured that their meaning is clear, at least not to us. Almost certainly each meant something then, to him, though even he will have been confused, have cursed his own hand, or have forgotten the intended import of a phrase after a time. Which goes to make them the more intimately his.

Of course, he has not made it easy. These diaries that put structure on his days, are simultaneously without structure, without a form that makes them readily accessible to us on the outside. In thousands of letters and notes, he tended to impose an order—managing and organising, hectoring and reproving—but these diaries are words in the midst of things. They are radically different to other sources on Michael Collins. They bring us nearer, closer than ever maybe, to the bustle of his life.

Consequently, this book is not another life of Michael Collins. It is, instead, a journey into the ravel of a source. It might have been a different book if he had left us contemplative diaries of the type historians use when they claim to see their subject's soul, but these are gnomic, cryptic, appointment books and demand a different approach. In the challenge of their form, he makes us look again.

His diaries change the angle of vision on Collins and the wider revolution. These little books, which ordered out his individual days, at once speed time up and slow it down. It is as if someone is showing us a newsreel, often too fast and then suddenly too slow. Amidst a maelstrom of work and effort come moments in stunning freeze-frame. We get the relentless pace of revolution, but also the slow grind of individual days. We see him interacting with so many people; he rushes about. Yet he experiences all of it in the midst of the quotidian, the personal, and the mundane.

In these diaries we see something he never intended us to see, his life in small, page-shaped blocks of intimate time. In the process, he gives us a revolution we do not usually encounter. Or, perhaps, one we have skipped too readily over in favour of the next instalment of Ireland's fighting story. Collins was integral to that story, but his diaries reveal a revolution of meetings and committees, of networks and connections carefully built, of money collected and appointments kept. It was hard, slow, repetitive work and the weapons that came most readily to him were paper, ink and a nib. These are the diaries of someone ascending through a revolution, but ascending through a bureaucracy as well. From buying cigarettes for the prisoners in Mountjoy to Downing Street and deciding the fate of a nation, he lived decades of experience in these short five years. His diaries show us, almost in real time, someone developing, from a revolutionary to a statesman. He begins the diaries as a paid office manager. By their end, he is leading a government.

This is a book of 21 short essays, each one an excursion into what the diaries let us see. Other historians would have made other choices but, with luck, some of ours will prove the joists and beams on which conversations rest. There are patterns yes, but always alongside the pulse and the mess, the contingent and the unresolved.

The last page we have is for a Sunday, 6 August 1922. It begins 'I Inspection Barracks today', and continues 'II Mass', before it ends 'III   '.[1] He seems farther away and closer to us in the words and in the gaps, in I and II but also III, the almost written down.

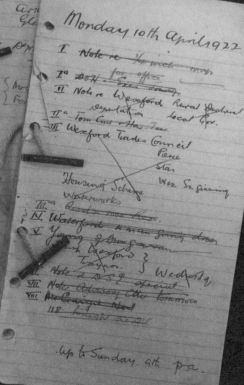

THE DIARIES

THE DIARIES

There are five.

The first is for 1918. T.J. & J. Smith Ltd of Charterhouse Square, London, produced it. Smith was a leading manufacturer and this one belonged to a range the company promoted as 'Automatic Self-Registering' diaries.

The defining gimmick was a steel spring which held his pencil in place, allowing it to double-job as a bookmark of wood and lead. This ensured, as the ads explained, 'The page last written upon immediately found on opening the Book, with Pencil ready to hand.'[1] The pocket diary market had been growing rapidly since the 1890s, encouraging companies like T. J. & J. Smith to produce an ever greater variety, designed and branded to meet a range of needs, an array of self-images.[2] This one said clever, business-like, practical; ideal for the busy office manager and revolutionary.

Unsurprisingly, Collins did not complete a page titled 'Personal Notes', leaving blank not simply his name, address, and telephone number, but his glove, collar, boot and hat size, as well as his height and weight. He did paste a listing of Irish MPs from 1916 inside the front cover. Keeping count, he struck through the departed, replacing each, in pen, with the by-election victor.

That diary was small, 12cm long, 7.5cm wide and less than a centimetre deep: snug in his hand and safe in his pocket. Each week laid out across facing pages, Sunday to Saturday in bold green print and in separate boxes, framed in red and lined in grey.

In 1919 he switched from a burgundy cover to red faux leather, and to a Collins' Gentleman's Diary No.174. It afforded him a page a day and, consequently, was slightly thicker but the purpose did not change. These diaries were functional and, in that sense only, essential. They did not give his life meaning. He did not interrogate himself nor did he explain himself to anyone else, instead these pages helped him to get to meetings on time, most of the time. Do not imagine careful compositions, products of pause and contemplation, but hurried notes, necessary lists, addresses, *aides-mémoire*, donations, calculations, things to do, things not done, accumulations, asides and abbreviations.

That page a day did give him more scope. The lists got longer. Did this reflect his changing life or the enhanced daily ration of diary lines? Either way, come 1920 he invested again in a Collins' Gentleman's diary. Exactly the same, but black. From September of that year, the entries became sparser, perhaps because life became hotter and a diary more dangerous.

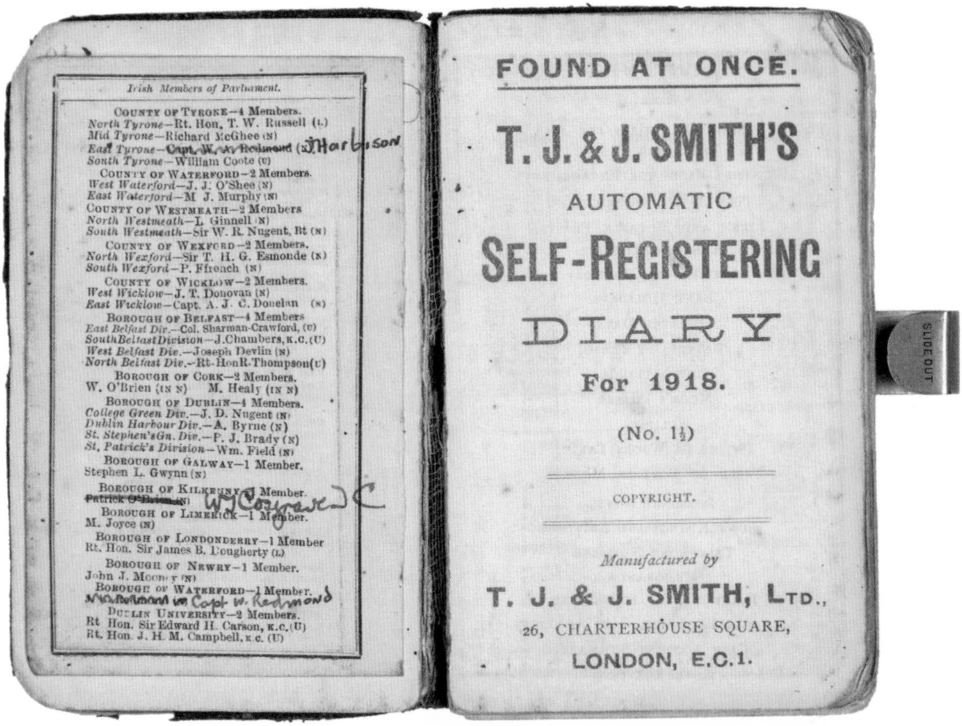
Irish Members of Parliament.
County of Tyrone—4 Members.
North Tyrone—Rt. Hon. T. W. Russell (L)
Mid Tyrone—Richard McGhee (N)
East Tyrone—Capt. W. A. Redmond (N) J. Harbison
South Tyrone—William Coote (U)
County of Waterford—2 Members.
West Waterford—J. J. O'Shee (N)
East Waterford—M. J. Murphy (N)
County of Westmeath—2 Members
North Westmeath—L. Ginnell (N)
South Westmeath—Sir W. R. Nugent, Bt (N)
County of Wexford—2 Members.
North Wexford—Sir T. H. G. Esmonde (N)
South Wexford—P. Ffrench (N)
County of Wicklow—2 Members.
West Wicklow—J. T. Donovan (N)
East Wicklow—Capt. A. J. C. Donelan (N)
Borough of Belfast—4 Members
East Belfast Div.—Col. Sharman-Crawford, (U)
South Belfast Division—J. Chambers, K.C. (U)
West Belfast Div.—Joseph Devlin (N)
North Belfast Div.—Rt. Hon R. Thompson (U)
Borough of Cork—2 Members.
W. O'Brien (IN N) M. Healy (IN N)
Borough of Dublin—4 Members.
College Green Div.—J. D. Nugent (N)
Dublin Harbour Div.—A. Byrne (N)
St. Stephen's Gn. Div.—P. J. Brady (N)
St. Patrick's Division—Wm. Field (N)
Borough of Galway—1 Member.
Stephen L. Gwynn (N)
Borough of Kilkenny—1 Member.
Patrick O'Brien (N) W. T. Cosgrave S.F.
Borough of Limerick—1 Member.
M. Joyce (N)
Borough of Londonderry—1 Member
Rt. Hon. Sir James B. Dougherty (L)
Borough of Newry—1 Member.
John J. Mooney (N)
Borough of Waterford—1 Member.
W. Redmond (N) Capt W. Redmond
Dublin University—2 Members.
Rt. Hon. Sir Edward H. Carson, K.C. (U)
Rt. Hon. J. H. M. Campbell, K.C. (U)
FOUND AT ONCE.
T. J. & J. SMITH'S
AUTOMATIC
SELF-REGISTERING
DIARY
For 1918.
(No. 1½)
COPYRIGHT.
Manufactured by
T. J. & J. SMITH, Ltd.,
26, CHARTERHOUSE SQUARE,
LONDON, E.C.1.
SLIDE OUT

↑
The 1918 Diary

Collins's T.J. & J. Smith diary for 1918, with its promise that all could be 'Found At Once'

National Archives, 2021/110/1

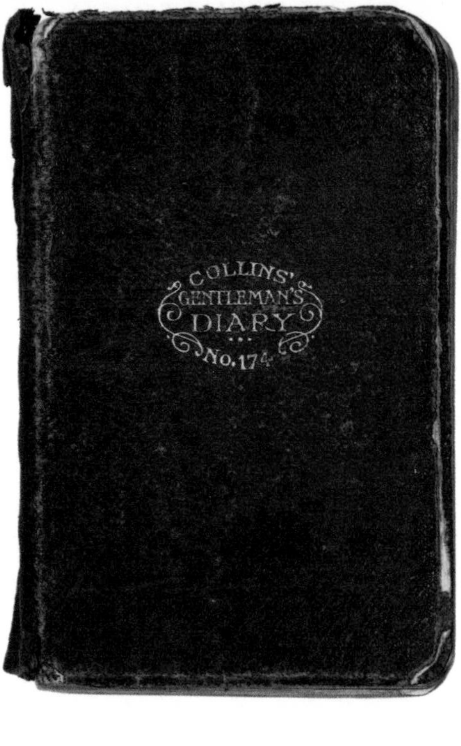
COLLINS'
GENTLEMAN'S
DIARY
No.174

→
The cover of his diary for 1919

National Archives, 2021/110/2

THE HOME AND COLONIAL TEA STORES
(FOR PRICES, SEE MIDDLE OF BOOK.)

Epithalamium — Nuptial song...
Equivocal — A word... of doubtful meaning
Erode — To wear away. to corrode
Erotic — An amorous poem
Erysipelas — An inflammatory disease of the skin
Escarpment — The precipitous side of a hill...
Escritoire — Writing desk
Esculent — Edible [Escarfood v Eto beat]
Espionage — Employment of... spies
Etching — ✗
Ethnology — Science of races.
Etymology — the history of words.
Euphemism — agreeable in sound.
Evanescent — Liable to vanish — Fleeting
Execrable — Disgraceful.
Exigency — Urgent, pressing necessity
Exodus — Departure etc.

← **A dictionary notebook**

Collins seems to have liked notebooks. As a young man in London, he kept one in which he created a personal dictionary. On this page, for instance, he defined 'euphemism' as 'agreeable in sound'.

UCD Archives, P123/14

Either he did not keep one for most of 1921, or we do not have it. Then, during the London negotiations, on Wednesday 12 October, regular entries resumed. From that day till the end he was at it again; noting, listing, recording on the somewhat larger pages of a more expensive notebook which he transformed into a diary by writing the day and date at the top.

Until that sudden stop.

→ **Collins at his desk**

Collins, photographed here during the Treaty negotiations in London in late 1921, was perhaps more familiar to his contemporaries in this pose than any other. Collins makes little sense without his papers and his desks.

National Library of Ireland, NPA POLF32

A DIARY SHAPED LIFE

A DIARY-SHAPED LIFE

Some years pass quicker than others. The Irish revolution rushes: the Rising, election, Dáil, war, truce, Treaty, split, civil war, end.

From 1923 time seems slower again; maybe in part because Collins was gone. In most tellings of the Irish revolution the work of months, years, contract into a sequence of dramatic episodes, and hindsight brings a momentum many who lived through 1916–23 might never have recognised. Revolutions make good stories, and Michael Collins above all kept the pages turning fast.

But Collins's five diaries stop this momentum in its tracks. His days, measured out in hours, in half-hours, in meetings and committees and so many letters sent, are each one long and full and followed by another just as long and just as full again. The working week of Monday to Saturday, borrowed many of his Sundays in 1918 and 1919; by 1921 Collins stole back only the odd day for himself.

Full as they are, the diaries of 1918 and 1919 reflect largely his 'second work day', the one that began when the staff in the many different offices he oversaw had gone home.[1] The diaries mostly record the times and places he needed to remember, not the steady grind of daily work. '8 O'C[lock] at 44, 8.30 at no 41', '6 O'C No 6 Election C[ommi]ttee. 8 [O'C] Organisation Cttee'; 6.00, 7.30, 8.00, 8.30 in one evening; 10.00, 10.30 at night; once two meetings at the same time—the diaries account for evenings filled, weekends travelling, money gathered.[2] They reflect the scale of Collins's voracious appetite for more and more work.

The diaries map him at addresses, and they put him on the clock. His weeks were shaped by those numbers, numbers that meant addresses: 6 was Harcourt Street and Sinn Féin headquarters; 32 was Bachelor's Walk and the office of the Irish National Aid and Volunteer Dependents' Fund (INA&VDF); 35 was Gardiner Street, an Irish Republican Brotherhood (IRB) meeting place; 44 was Mountjoy Street, a place to gather, a home of sorts for a while.[3] There were other numbers, and, like the initials, they signified just enough to remind him of where he needed to be and who he was to meet. The slightly worried, perhaps exasperated, 'Mtg today @ where?' of 10 September 1920 was a rare case of Collins losing track.[4] As 1921 became 1922 phone numbers meant people, particularly in London, but in Dublin too. He worked in a world of initials, of first names, and in the pages of his diaries some names recur while others come and go, important for a time, but quickly overtaken by the urgency of other things.

Monday 6th March 1922

I Wrote Clement Shorter re Memorial
II " Sean Nunan.
III " Sean MacCaoIlte,
IV " Piaras Beaslaí.
V Return Gold watch Johnston
VI Redeemed docked for last week
VII Note to Sean McKeon re Cork
VIII " re Seamus Hogan for
        seeing Michael Hogan }
IX Catalogue library
X Able to Blythe. re figures
XI " re Athlone meeting or
XII   Roscommon re license
XIII To speak M. O. re Report Seanties.
        (a) Phone
      \   (b) Cars   (c) Money.
        (d) Guns   (e) Receipts also.

Diary, 6 March 1922

By then head of the Provisional Government, his diary entries had become longer,
with lists each day of people to meet and always so much to be done.

National Archives, 2021/110/5

**Diary, 6–12
January 1918**

A typical busy week full
of initials, abbreviations
and numbers.

National Archives,
2021/110/1

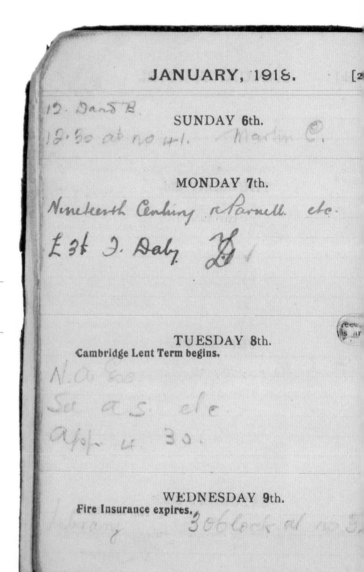

JANUARY, 1918.   [2

SUNDAY 6th.

MONDAY 7th.

TUESDAY 8th.
Cambridge Lent Term begins.

WEDNESDAY 9th.
Fire Insurance expires.

𝔈piphany.

THURSDAY 10th

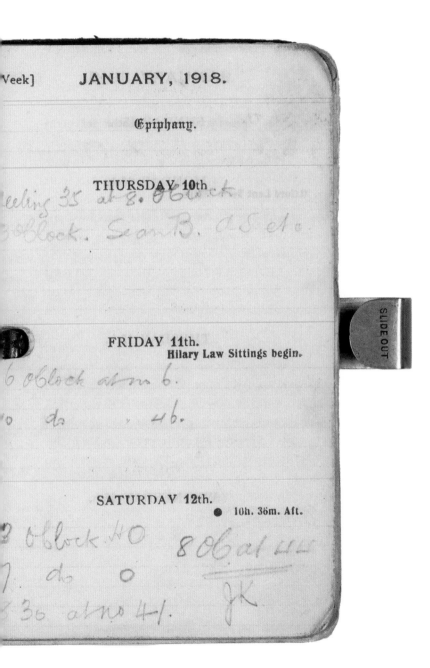

eeling 35 at 8. o'clock

o'block. Sean B. c.S etc.

FRIDAY 11th.
Hilary Law Sittings begin.

6 o'block at no 6.

o   do   . 4b.

SATURDAY 12th.
● 10h. 36m. Aft.

3 o'block #O   806 at use

7. do   o

30 at no 4 .   JK

19

When the diaries began Collins was 27, prominent in republican circles, but not yet in the public eye. He was a member of the Sinn Féin Executive, secretary of the supreme council of the IRB and director of organisation of the Irish Volunteers. As he became by turn over the years a member of the Sinn Féin standing committee, a TD, a member of the cabinet, minister for finance, president of the IRB, director of intelligence of the Irish Volunteers, acting president of the Dáil, a plenipotentiary to negotiations, chairman of the Provisional Government, commander-in-chief of the new National Army, each title brought its own work, its own mountains of paper, its own frustrations, and more colleagues to be exasperated by. But though the character of his work changed as he became more powerful through these five years, although the meetings in Harcourt Street and Gardiner Street became conferences in Downing Street, meetings in the House of Lords, the diaries show steady consistencies alongside the obvious dramatic shifts.[5] On 8 March 1922 he made note of a Mr Kelly in Mullingar. There was a job at the railway station to see about.[6] On 1 August 1922 he reminded himself to send a note to the quartermaster about army mattresses.[7] While these entries speak of a man still reluctant to delegate in 1922, they spoke too of that old instinct that never lost sight of the smallest thing even when there was a provisional government to run and a civil war to be won.

The diaries are full of work, work that from 1921 now meant portraits to sit for and journalists to impress, work that now meant split and civil war and all the burden of that. But alongside work there were the comforts and obligations of family—sisters' letters to answer, a doctor's appointment to be made for his brother Seán.[8] There was football to be watched, the odd play to be seen, his own expenses to be claimed and the dentist to be endured. And there were better things. There was a life starting with Kitty Kiernan; there was a future to plan. The diaries were the sum of so much to be done.

A make-shift office

The diaries sometimes don't give us what we might expect. We are often left, like the photographer here, with a busy table and an empty chair.

National Library of Ireland, Ms 40,431/3

ABSENCES

ABSENCES

There is a lot that isn't there; things that don't get mentioned, names that don't appear. He writes nothing of becoming a TD, a cabinet minister, nothing about Soloheadbeg or the meeting of the first Dáil. He becomes director of intelligence without comment, and makes no note of the first or any other shootings by The Squad. Silent for some of the hardest months, the 1921 diary only begins in October in London, and falls quiet two days before the Treaty was signed: 6 December passes without remark. The Dáil voted on the Treaty, he became chairman of the Provisional Government, he agreed two pacts with the Northern Ireland Premier Sir James Craig, Sir Henry Wilson was killed, all without a word from Collins in his diaries, not a word.

If we see these and his many other silences in the diaries as significant gaps, then perhaps more fool us. An empty 6 December 1921 is a sharp reminder, if one were needed, that his five diaries were chiefly engagement books, to-do lists; they were neither 'a companion or a confidant', not the place to pour out his heart, not the last piece in the Collins puzzle for us to solve.[1] The very different diary he kept during his brief time in Sligo Gaol is further proof. He had read his Mitchel and his Clarke well enough to know a pocket diary with such small spaces for each passing day was not up to the gaol journal job. The 'big Diary' he refers to in February 1922 confirms that his own 1922 diary was a private supplement to a more official appointment book.[2] His five pocket diaries were largely notes of the things he needed to remember, and that doesn't necessarily make them repositories of the most important things. He knew he'd signed the Treaty; he didn't need to write it down.

Rather than conceive of his silences as missing parts, perhaps we need a different angle of approach. If we understand Collins as an extraordinary figure living through an extraordinary time, the diaries are something of a jolt. That familiar chronology that rushes through the revolution, that carries Collins swiftly from one significant moment to the next is, in these diaries, slowed down to the pace of a day, and each day comes as likely concerned with his ordinary as well as his remarkable life. On 5 August 1922 he made a note amongst other things to get 'Knickers', 'White Collars' and 'Socks'.[3] That morning the newspapers were full of the funeral of Harry Boland, but there was no mention in his diary of his friend's death.[4] We might choose to read that silence as callous, but Collins

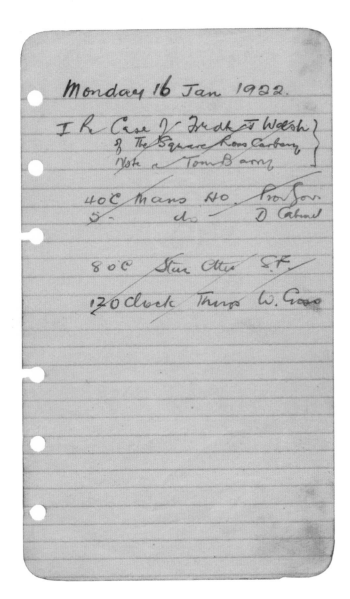

Diary, 16 January 1922

The Provisional Government recorded in the minutes of its first meeting at 11am on 16 January 1922 that 'Arrangements were made to visit Dublin Castle at 1.40pm in the afternoon for the purpose of taking over the various Departments of State'. Though Collins was heard afterwards remarking 'Griffith! The Castle has fallen!' he made no note of it here.

National Archives, 2021/110/5

NOVEMBER, 1918.   [46th

Ans Katie Kelly Mary.

SUNDAY 10th.   *Finn Sealy*

MONDAY 11th.
☽ 4h. 46m. Aft.
Half Quarter Day.

*Black re Gavan D & Engus
& 2 copies
2 maps to Horgan   Skib
Armistice announced.*

TUESDAY 12th.

*Art . San & Sean.
also to Sean asking for
return of goods.*

WEDNESDAY 13th.

Diary, 11 November 1918

This day's entry embodies the mix of the momentous and the
mundane that runs throughout the diaries.

National Archives, 2021/110/1

MAY, 1918.

Sunday after Ascension

THURSDAY 16th.

See Sean after arrival

7 at No 6.

FRIDAY 17th.
☽ 8h. 14m. Aft.
Oxford Easter Term ends.
Easter Law Sittings end.

See Gnm. Arrest of Mary S ?
Sarah detained .
8 at ʜʜ H. Q. at n? ?
lodgings + eluded
them

SATURDAY 18th.
Oxford Trinity Term begins.

41 at 8 06 Appointments not
entered after the
date as I'll be
on the run

Diary, 17–18 May 1918

While he may have congratulated himself on evading arrest, there
quickly came the blunt reality of going on the run.

National Archives, 2021/110/1

wrote of Boland's loss, of his own remorse, in a more fitting place.[5] So maybe it's our assumptions that need to readjust. His diary isn't silent; rather those August pages hum with how he filled those harrowing days.

The diaries are full of names, but names are rarely constant; people come and go, and there is that same scope to read more than we might into the gaps. Names we might instinctively associate with Collins, Liam Tobin, Tom Cullen, Joe O'Reilly, Richard Mulcahy; individuals who later wrote of themselves as Collins's closest confidants, Piaras Béaslaí, David Neligan, or Batt O'Connor, make fleeting, infrequent appearances, and left to the diaries alone, one might question how much they really were 'with Michael Collins in the fight for Irish independence'.[6] But they, like so many others, were perhaps so essential, so ubiquitous, why would he bother to write their names down. As 1919 moved into 1920 he must have been mindful of the consequences of his diaries being captured, that any name written was at risk. But apparent gaps had other causes too. Austin Stack is there through 1918 and 1919, but as Collins's responsibilities changed, Stack's name all but disappeared. 'Mrs deV.' appears in the diaries as often as her husband, but it would be unwise to assume Éamon de Valera wasn't on his mind.[7]

Maybe because he wrote them so rarely, his direct notes of momentous moments stand more starkly out. And why he chose what he chose is open to surmise. In response to the 'German Plot' arrests of mid-May 1918, he wrote 'Arrest of Many S.F. Saw the detectives at my own lodgings & eluded them'.[8] The following day he added a rather naïve postscript: 'appointments not entered after this date as I'll be on the run'.[9] For several weeks after he wrote each day the letter R for run. These entries might reflect a new urgency, a new danger, to what he was doing, but it wasn't long before those 'appointments' crept back in again. He recorded the global as well as local. Like many around the world he noted the armistice on 11 November 1918, though he spelt it as many said it 'Armstice',

At the Gresham Hotel, Dublin the night the Dáil ratified the Treaty, 7 January 1922

No diary entry exists for 7 January 1922, but there is plenty of weary relief in this pose.

National Library of Ireland, HOGW 126

and on 28 June the following year, the Treaty of Versailles appeared with 'Peace was signed at 3.15pm today'.[10] 'Made Ministerial Statement on Finance' on 9 May 1919 maybe says something of the personal pride, the relief of giving his first important speech to a Dáil meeting as Minister for Finance.[11] 'M.C. c in c' was his more muted response to becoming head of the army in the opening weeks of civil war.[12] His note of 29 June 1922 'Attack on Four Courts Contd' is spare enough to be a statement of fact, but its brevity might just as well reveal a heavy heart.[13]

Written in fragments more often than sentences, the temptation is to put a sense that suits us on what he writes.[14] His silences might well discommode us, but in these notes, written in the passing of a moment, he remains a Collins who refuses to be pinned down.

Hannie and Seán Collins at Michael Collins's grave, Glasnevin Cemetery, August 1922

In 1923 Hannie wrote 'how changed and cold and lonely the world without him is for his friends, and above all for me'.

FAMILY

FAMILY

His family life had its rhythms much like his working week. Sunday seemed to be his day for writing home, a habit perhaps formed young in London, and maintained at least through 1918 and 1919.[1] Home was people as much as a place; home meant his sisters Katie and Mary, his sister-in-law Katty, but home most often meant Hannie, the sister whom he had lived and grown up with in London, the one who knew the man he had turned into best.[2] The arrival of a letter from Hannie was worth noting in his diary, and the disappointment of her not arriving in Dublin as planned in May 1919 was certainly remarked.[3] She appeared in the diary through his time in London in 1921, and he saw her again when he returned there in early 1922.[4] As in any family some siblings stay closer than others; the address in Chicago for 'P.J. Collins', scribbled at the back of the 1920 diary, suggests the stranger his brother Patrick had become.[5] 'We thought alike on many subjects', Hannie remembered. It was obvious for those who knew them in those early London days, they were simply 'the closest of chums'.[6]

His diaries intimate that he thought of home at those times when home was most certain to be missed. On Sunday 13 April 1919 he 'Wrote Hannie, Katie Celestine Kattie'.[7] The 14 April was the anniversary of his mother's death.[8] And he went home at those times when families were supposed to gather: for Saint Patrick's Day, for Easter in 1918, for the new year and in the summer of 1919, for Christmas as the Dáil tore itself apart in 1921, for Saint Patrick's Day again in 1922.[9] Of course, when he went to Cork, there were collections to be made, speeches to give, elections to canvas for, but the diary entry 'To Cork. Dunmanway by Car to Clon[akilty]', ended with the one resonant word 'Home'.[10] It might be the place he grew out of and grew beyond, but he hankered at the obvious times for Cork, for Woodfield, for home.

As the youngest of eight, Collins had grown up as 'Baby' to his siblings, and while he remained that to his sister Helena who last saw him before entering a convent in 1901, the boy who had been 'Tom Tulliver' to his sister Katie, had become the most powerful man in the country by 1921.[11] How that changed his family's sense of him is impossible to know, but his diaries show him taking on new responsibilities for his siblings as the years went on. On 9 November 1919 Collins 'Wrote Mary re Finances etc'.[12] Mary was nine years older than him; she had nine children and had become a widow just one month before.[13] Mary once wrote that 'All the news I ever got from Michael was from the papers', but

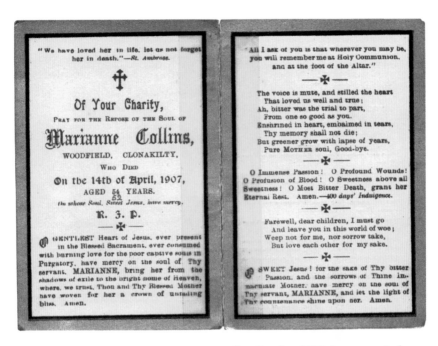

Memorial card for Collins's mother, Marianne

Collins was almost a year in London when his mother died in 1907. He kept this reminder of his mother with him for the rest of his life.

Courtesy of the Michael Collins House Museum, Clonakilty

after October 1919 that seems to have changed, he 'had been helping her with gifts and cash and in kind', and 'had promised her that he would afford her considerable help in maintaining herself and her children and in educating the latter'.[14] She received a dependant's allowance from the Military Service Pension Board on that basis in 1954.[15] On 29 January 1922 Collins wrote in his diary 'Note re Claire Powell'.[16] Claire Powell was Mary's daughter and was then fourteen.[17] Having the attention of the head of the Provisional Government would have given a niece a good start.

Johnny Collins, and he remained Johnny rather than Seán in his brother's diaries, featured differently in their pages in 1922 than in earlier years.[18] Before, he was the recipient of letters but on 21 March 1922 Collins wrote 'Note re Johnnie's claim & Registering same', helping his brother to apply, perhaps, for compensation for the destruction of Woodfield.[19] Collins must have felt the loss of his home badly, must have imagined it was targeted as a way to get to him. It

Palm
Sunday. Sunday 13

Hugh Bp today at 2.3

Wrote
Hannie,
Katie
Celestine
Kattie.

Whelan did not turn
up.

APRIL, 1919.

Monday 14

6 Ex at No 6.

Salary P.S. & Sean.

Frank Daly this eve at
Harcourt St.
Dick Stokes too

Wrote Austin
reply to his dated 9.4.19.

All points covered

Stopped
Cigarets today }

**Diary, 13
April 1919**

Sunday was often
the day for writing
family letters, and
the Sunday before his
mother's anniversary
he was clearly
thinking of home.

**National Archives,
2021/110/2**

File No. ____/____/____

Mrs. Mary Powell, Mount Carmel, Magazine Rd., Cork

D.P. 23755.

With regard to her present circumstances, claimant submits that her claim should be ~~struck~~ determined on the basis of her dependancy on her brother at the time of his death, and that her present circumstances should not enter into the case.

Claimant's husband died on 4/10/1919. Claimant informs me that at that time her deceased brother was Minister for Finance in Dáil Eireann, Director of Intelligence in the I.R.A., and Head Centre of the Irish Republican Brotherhood. At the time of his death he was Chairman of the Provisional Government and Commander-in-Chief of the National Army. From the time of her husband's death, deceased has been helping

Only one side of this paper is to be written upon.   Enclosure No.

File No. ..../......./........

her with gifts in cash and
in kind. Deceased had promised
her that he would afford her
considerable help in maintaining
herself and her children and
in educating the latter.

Claimant informs me that
after her brothers funeral, Mr.
Wm Cosgrave, who was subsequently
President of the Executive Council
of the Irish Free State, offered to
place a bill before Dail
Eireann to provide for claimant
+ her children (as was done for
the dependents of the late Arthur
Griffith). Claimant refused the
offer, despite her needs, for
idealistic reasons, and went
to work early in 1923 to provide
for herself + her children.

D E Buckley

Report by D.E. Buckley
of a meeting with
Mary Collins Powell,
10 February 1954

Along with so many
other changes in his
life, Collins's roles and
responsibilities within
his family altered across
the years of his diaries.

Military Archives,
Military Service
Pension Collection,
DP23755

had become dangerous to be the sibling of Michael Collins and he knew Johnny had paid a heavy price. In April 1922 Collins sought a doctor for Johnny's pains, and by 16 May he made note of a 'Gun for Johnny & 50 rounds'.[20] In 1964 Seán Collins told the *Sunday Independent* that his brother 'would do anything I asked him to do', and the diaries do suggest that he did try.[21] 'I was more than twelve years older than he was', Seán said, but it seems clear, even from these spare diaries, that when he became the notorious Michael Collins his place in that family fundamentally transformed.[22] 'Baby' had grown up and changed them all.

↑
Standing in the ruins of Woodfield with Seán Collins

Collins described the destruction of Woodfield: 'The dwelling house itself, and every out-office (with the exception of one stable) were completely destroyed...The net result therefore was that eight young children [Seán's family] were left homeless... To complete the story my brother, himself, was arrested...'

National Library of Ireland, INDH396

→
Elderly Sinn Féin supporters

Famously, Sinn Féin was associated with a rising generation whereas the Irish Party drew more support from the old. These gentlemen were, however, swept up in the enthusiasm for Sinn Féin.

National Library of Ireland, KE152

'ELECTION EXCITEMENT'

'ELECTION EXCITEMENT'

In 2011 Adam's auctioneers in Dublin sold several letters Collins sent to his sister Hannie. His diary records that he wrote to her on 1 December 1918,[1] and that one was among the auctioned batch. It fetched €8,500. Toward the end of the letter, Collins professed that the general 'election excitement', then approaching a peak, was not his priority. Sinn Féin was set for a transformative win, yet he suggested to Hannie that the 'turmoil' of the 'Political end . . . leaves me almost unmoved'.[2]

This was a common pose among a certain clique of Collins's colleagues, and one he had mocked gently just three days earlier when he wrote to 'Austin' Stack.[3] He was, he joked, having 'a quiet laugh' at the 'political eagerness of some of the "I'm only a fighting man" fraternity'.[4] The manner in which Collins opened his letter to Hannie emphasises the extent to which he was not only excited by political developments but at the heart of them:

> At the present moment things here are in such a rush that literally one hasn't a moment to give a calm thought nor a calm word. At Central HQ here in Dublin we are positively in a state of siege—morning noon and night callers callers callers all clamouring for speakers and assistance. Will do very well in the elections—the [Irish Parliamentary] Party is disintegrating, and every day bring[s] its fresh batch of seceders.[5]

His diary of 1918 reveals something of the work involved over a longer term. The first entry of the new year—'Make announcement at Mansion House. South City Concert'[6]—suggests he was there on 1 January when Count Plunkett told an event, organised by the Thomas MacDonagh Sinn Féin club, that the party had declared for 'complete independence' in the form of 'a republic' and would seek a seat at the peace conference.[7]

Mid-January brought a by-election campaign in South Armagh,[8] prompting '6 O'Clock Organising Cttee Sinn Fein' (18 January), 'Election sub-cttee at 4' (21 January), '5 O'Clock Election Cttee' (23 January) and '5 O'Clock at No.6 Election Cttee' (25 January). The following week he travelled north to campaign and we can track his itinerary: 'Armagh SF Club' (29 January), 'Belleek Dundalk' (30 January), 'Meeting Clady Whitecross' (31 January) and 'Polling South Armagh sub-agent at Clady Milltown' (1 February). The following day *The Irish Times* reported that 'the unfortunate voter had to pass through a regular barrage of fire from the literature guns as he went to his polling booth.'[9] It was, however, to no avail, and Collins recorded the disappointing, if expected, defeat of their candidate Patrick McCartan.[10]

The Waterford by-election of March intruded to a lesser extent. John Redmond's death on 6 March, which prompted that contest, went unremarked but Collins did record a flurry of election committee meetings, beginning on 8 March.[11] The result also features, but there is no sign that he travelled south to campaign.[12] Subsequent by-elections, including Arthur Griffith's victory in East Cavan in June, leave minimal or no trace, though in the month leading up to that contest he committed very little at all to the diaries. He was, after all, on the 'R[un]' since the arrest of many of his senior party colleagues in mid-May.[13]

The vacancies created by those arrests saw Collins elevated to membership of Sinn Féin's Standing Committee, the party's key decision-making body. His first meeting took place on 21 May but, in the months that followed, Collins did not always attend. Even when he did (as detailed in the minutes) the meetings do not necessarily appear in the diary.[14] He did note, 'Wrote SF S Cttee re O'Mahony' on 8 July, and the minutes of that evening confirm that the committee discussed the letter in which Collins complained 'of the meagerness & inadequacy of the allowance of £2 allowed to Mrs P.C. O'Mahony (wife of one of our prisoners) during her husband's imprisonment'.[15]

In September, the Standing Committee began the task of selecting the party's slate of candidates for a general election everyone knew was coming. Collins wanted, and got, the nomination for Cork South.[16] Signs of Collins's manoeuvres to secure this include correspondence with his brother: 'Wrote Johnny re South Cork in reply to his'.[17] Helpfully, Johnny was on the constituency executive.

Three months later, in that letter to Hannie, Collins allowed himself a little self-congulation: 'In all probability I'll go to Cork for the Nominations but am not certain, for the few of us (who have had practically the whole responsibility for the past 6 months) can't very well afford to get landed [arrested] at this stage. Even so we haven't done badly.'[18]

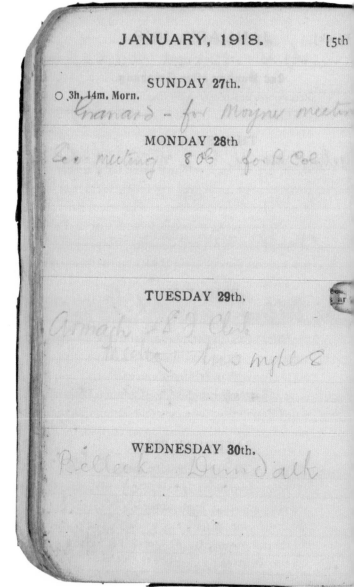

SUNDAY 27th.

○ 3h, 14m, Morn.

Granard – for Moyne meeting

MONDAY 28th

Co. meeting 8 06   for A Col.

**Diary, 27 January –
2 February 1918**

During his busy week in
Armagh, Collins noted the
anniversary of the Catholic
martyr Conor O'Devany,
though the seventeenth-
century bishop of Down
and Conor was executed
in 1612, not 1611.

National Archives,
2021/110/1

TUESDAY 29th.

Armagh F J Club
Meeting this night 8

WEDNESDAY 30th.

Belfast Dundalk

Septuagesima Sunday.

THURSDAY 31st,

about meeting of Leinstr.

...cting Cla dy   White cross

FRIDAY 1st,
FEBRUARY,

Brigid died at Kildare 525
nor O'Durany Bishop 9 poor Com...
...cutes 1611   Polling South
...maght sub agent at
...ady mc Cown   *JK.*

SATURDAY 2nd,

C. D. Cam og Guilde
Banba Doll. af 800.

Declaration of Poll S Armagh
Donnelly   2324
McCartan   1305
Richardson   40

South Armagh

Receipts

	£	s	d
Cheque to J. Boland	111	4	8
J. O'Connor + Mulcahy	60		
J. McGuinness	50		
Q. Stack	350		
J. M. Stanley	1	12	4
M. Collins	40		
P. Milroy	25		
R. Ginnell	300		
McQuaid	445		
M. Staines	1095		
J. Nunan	25		
Belfast Executive Loan	25		
Subscriptions collected by Belfast Executive	236	7	3
	276	4	4
Cash due to T. L. Fleming	1	15	
V. Cosgrave	10		
McCullogh for Cosgrave	170		
	2765	19	
	180		

42

ᴅo ṁuıɴɴċıʀ ᴅeıscıʀᴛ ċoʀcaıᵹe.

Ꝼo the Electors of South Cork.

Ꞇá opaıᵭ ᴅuıne ᴛoᵹaᵭ ꝼan Ollᴛoᵹaᵭ ꝼo ċuᵹaınn a ċuıꝼꝼıᵭ ı n-uṁaıl
ᴅon ᴛpaoᵹal caᵭ ıꝼ ᴛoıl lıᵭ ı ᴅᴛaoᵭ
náıpıᵭın na h-Ꞓıpeann.

Iappaım-ꝼe opaıᵭ mıpe ᴛoᵹaᵭ; aᵹuꝼ
nı aꝼ mo ꝼon ꝼéın ıappaımꝼe opaıᵭ é
aċ ᴛoıpc ᵹo ᵭꝼuılım aꝼ ᴛaoᵭ neaṁ-
ꝼpleaᴛċaıꝼ na h-Ꞓıpeann. Ꞇuᵹaıᵭ ᵭuꝼ
nᵹuᴛanna aꝼ ᴛaoᵭ na ꝼaoıpꝼe.

Iꝼı an ċeıpc aᴛá le ꝼocꝼú, ná, cıaca
ꝼaoppaꝼ Ꞓıpe nó ná ꝼaoppaꝼ í. Ꞇá
opaıᵭpe ᵭuꝼ ᵹcıon ꝼéın ᴅen ꝼocaꝼú
ꝼın a ᵭeunaṁ ꝼan ollᴛoᵹaᵭ ꝼo. Ꞇá
opaıᵭ a ċuꝼ ı nuṁaıl ᴅo náıpıúnaıᵭ
an ᴅoṁaın, le nᵭuꝼ nᵹuᴛanna, ᵹo
n-éılıᵹeann muınnᴛıꝼ na h-Ꞓıpeann
ıomlán ꝼaoıppe ıꝼ neaṁpoleaᴅċaıꝼ
aᵹuꝼ ná ᵭeımıᵭ ꝼápca le héınnıú
nıoꝼ luᵹa ná ꝼon, aᵹuꝼ éın pleaın nó
ᴛıonnpcnaıṁ ꝼıaᵹlᴛaıꝼ ná ꝼáᵹaıᵭ an ċoṁaċc aᵹuꝼ an
ꝼmáċc aꝼ ꝼaᵭ ꝼé ṁuınnᴛıꝼ na ᴛıꝼe ı nᵹaᵭ nıᵭ a
ᵭaıneann le ᵹnóċaı na ᴛıꝼe ı néıꝼınn aᵹuꝼ caꝼ leaꝼ,
ná ꝼuıl ann aċ ċúıꝼ ṁaᵹaıᵭ ᵹan ᵭpıᵹ ᵹan éıpeaċc.
Ꞇá opaıᵭ a ᵭeapᵭú ᴅon ᴛpaoᵹal ıe neaꝼc ᵭuꝼ
nᵹuᴛanna ᵹuꝼ ᴅ'aıṁᵭeoın muınnᴛıꝼe na h-Ꞓıpeann
aċoımeaᴅann Sapana an ᴛıꝼ ꝼeo ꝼé ꝼmáċc, aᵹuꝼ na
ꝼuıl ᴅe ᵭunúꝼ le n-a péıṁ ꝼan ꝼeo aċ Láıṁ Láıᴅıꝼ
aᵹuꝼ ꝼóıꝼéıᵹean, ᵹan ceaᴅ ᵭúınn-na, aᵹuꝼ ᵹo
ꝼcuıꝼꝼımıᵭ puaꝼ ᴅon ꝼmáċc ᵹallᴅa.
Ꝺoncuıᵹım le ᴛuaıpmı luċc "Sınn Ꝼeın." Má
ᴛoᵹann pıᵭ mıpe maꝼ ꝼeıpıꝼe, ᴅeapᵭuıᵹım ná ꝼaᵹaᵭ
ᵹo ᴅcı Paꝼlaımenᴛ Sapana, maꝼ ıꝼ ıonann ᴅul ann
aᵹuꝼ aᴅṁáıl ᵹo ᵭꝼuıl ꝼoᵹaꝼ ceıᴅıl aᵹ Sapana cun
an ᴛıꝼ ꝼeo a ꝼıaᵹlú. Iꝼ coıꝼ ı n-aᵹaıᵭ an cıpc ᴅul
ᵹo ᴅcı Paꝼlaımenᴛ Sapana, aᵹuꝼ ᴅá ṁıpcıᵭe an ᴛıꝼ
ꝼeıꝼpı na h-Ꞓıpeann ᴅo ᴅul ann. Ꝺeaᵭ Ꞓıpe ı n-uṁaꝼ
na haımıléıpe ᵭá ᵭáꝼꝼ, maꝼa mᵭeaᵭ ꝼé ᵭuıne ᵭeuᵹ
ᴅeꝼ na h-Ꞓıpeannaıᵹ ᵭa ċpoᵭa aᵹuꝼ ᴅoᵭ uaıꝼle áꝼ
cáınıᵹ cun ᵭaıl ꝼıaṁ, ᴅo ċpeopuıᵹ muınnᴛıꝼ na
h-Ꞓıpeann ó ᵭealaċ a mᵭaꝼcᴛa cꝼ⸱n-a mᵭáꝼ calma.
Oꝼ ꝼuᴅ é ᵹuꝼ ᴅóıċ lıom ná ꝼuıl ᴅ⸱ ċeıpc aᵹaıꝼ ı le
péıᴅıeaċ ꝼan Ollᴛoᵹaᵭ aċ cıaca ꝼaoppaꝼ Ꞓıpe ı ó ná
ꝼaoppaꝼ í, nı ᵹáᵭ ᵭoṁ ᴛpáċc aꝼ a ᵭꝼuıl ᵭeapcuıᵹce
aᵹ luċc Sınn Ꝼéın le ᴅeunaṁ aꝼ ꝼan leaꝼa na ᴛıꝼe.
Claoıᵭım le ᴛuaıpım Ꝺulꝼ Ꞇeon, a ᴅuᵭaıꝼc:—
" Ꞇıopánᴛaċᴛ an Rıaᵹalᴛaıꝼ ᵹallᴅa ṁalluıᵹce
ᴅo ċuꝼ aꝼ ceal, ᴅeıꝼe a ċuꝼ le n-áꝼ ᵹcomċean-
ᵹaılc ᴅe Sapana—ꝼuᴅ na ᵭun le n-áꝼ n-acꝼaı
ᵹo léıꝼ—aᵹuꝼ neaṁpleaᴅċoꝼ na h-Ꞓıpeann ᴅo
ċuꝼ ı n-áıpıċe ᵭúınn—ꝼın a ꝼaıᵭ uaım !"

Sın a ᵭꝼuıl uaım-ꝼe leıꝼ.
Mıpe,

"ʃᴛaʀ" Skibbereen.

Michael Collins

You will be asked in the coming General Election to choose a person who
will represent you in the public life of the
Nation.

In seeking your votes I do so for no
personal motive, but on the broad general ground that I stand for the Sovereign
Independence of Ireland. I ask you by
your votes to endorse that stand.

The issue at stake is whether Ireland
is or **is not** to be free. You, as part of
the Irish Electorate, are asked to help in
the decision. You are requested, by your
votes, to assert before the Nations of the
world that Ireland's claim is to the status
of an Independent Nation, and that we
shall be satisfied with nothing less than
our full claim—that in fact aɪy
scheme of Government which does
not confer upon the people of Ireland the
supreme, absolute, and final control of all
this country, external as well as internal, is
a mockery and will not be accepted.

You are asked, by your votes, to re-affirm that England
holds this country against the wishes of the
Irish people, and that her continued occupation of our
country is due solely to her superior brute force, and re-
ceives no sanction from us, that we protest against that
occupation, and against England's usurpation of our National Right to Rule ourselves.

I appear before you in cordial agreement with the doc-
trines of Sinn Fein, and if you elect me as your Representative, I pledge myself **not** to attend the British Parliament, as I hold that attendance in that hostile assembly
gives a show of legality to England's unjust claim to rule
this country. Holding this view, I believe attendance
there to be **wrong in principle, in practice it
has proved a ghastly failure,** and had
well-nigh landed us in disaster, until sixteen of
the noblest men, that this or any gener-
ation in Ireland produced, by their calm and unflinching
self-sacrifice, redeemed the National situation.

Believing as I do, that the issue at the Election is the
Independence of this country, it is not necessary to outline
the ameliorative social programme of Sinn Fein. I accept
the dictum laid down over a century ago by Wolfe Tone:—

"TO SUBVERT THE TYRANNY OF OUR EXE-
CRABLE GOVERNMENT, TO BREAK THE CON-
NECTION OF ENGLAND — **THE UNFAILING
SOURCE OF ALL OUR ILLS**—AND TO ASSERT
THE INDEPENDENCE OF MY NATIVE COUNTRY
—THESE WERE MY OBJECTS."

TO-DAY THESE ARE MY OBJECTS.

To The Electors of South Cork

Though Collins would take the South Cork seat without a contest, he did issue an election address in
which he emphasised his republican credentials by concluding with a quotation from Wolfe Tone.

National Library of Ireland, Ms 40,422/5

43

Election handbill South Armagh by-election

In this handbill Sinn Féin borrowed a cartoon by Bert Wilton Williams of *London Opinion* to imply that, in contrast to Carson and Redmond, Patrick McCartan could be relied on to oppose conscription.

National Library of Ireland, EPH C473a

Tom Cullen

Tom Cullen was one of Collins's closest associates. He worked on the importation of arms and was a senior figure on Collins's intelligence staff.

National Library of Ireland, BEA50

ASSOCIATION

The Irish Republican Brotherhood (IRB) was a political ambition and an instrument of revolution. The very name calls to mind conspiracy, violence and a certain attitude to the world. Depending on your point of view, it was an identity forged in social activity, an elite version of patriotic Irish manliness, a vampire feeding on the organisations built by others, an anti-democratic menace, or all of these.[1] It was also a feeling of solidarity: it was sentiment and obligation.

On Tuesday, 5 March 1918 Michael Collins wrote in his diaries, 'Removal of Mattie Murphy 3 O'Clock from Mater H[ospital] to Fairview chapel' and, on the next day, 'Funeral of Mattie Murphy at 3 O'C.'[2] The *Irish Independent* reported that 'several companies of Volunteers' attended the removal and that the 'coffin was draped with republican colours.' Murphy was, the headline said, 'A '67 Man Dead'.[3] Few obscure old Fenians received quite so grand a send-off (Mattie Murphy was no Jeremiah O'Donovan Rossa) and no other features in this way in Michael Collins's diaries. But then Mattie Murphy—widower, weaver, retired to Artane—was the father to John Murphy and John carried the tradition.[4] It had taken him to raid the Magazine Fort at Phoenix Park on Easter Week 1916, and into Stafford Gaol and Frongoch Camp with Michael Collins.[5]

The secretive IRB is everywhere in the diaries: sometimes in ways it should not be. During 1919 Collins regularly took the roll of what seem to have been the meetings of his circle.[6] For example, on 24 April 1919 he noted that 26 were present, 7 excused and 2 absent. More than that, he wrote, 'Elected M. Collins O[,] J. Nunan Sec. Joe Furlong Treas.'[7] That 'O' was, presumably, his symbol for centre, head of the revolutionary cell. Seán Nunan and Joe Furlong, along with Joe's brother Matt, had been companions of Collins since the London days and had participated in the Rising.[8] Nunan would tour America with de Valera (is the imperative 'Send Sean Nunan' of 8 May 1919 a reference to this?)[9] and Matt Furlong would die on 15 October 1920, following an accident while testing a mortar.[10] It was the product of a basement bomb factory, hidden under the apparently innocent Heron & Lawless bicycle shop at 198 Parnell Street.[11]

Thursday 24

Tom Cullen DI Suspended from Co transferred with Engineers.

Roll 35 Elected
Pres 26 ⎫ M. Collins O
Sec 7 ⎬ J Nunan Sec.
Abs 2 ⎭ Joe Furlong Treas.

Subs:- 30/= $\frac{1-8}{9}$ $\frac{d}{4}$ taken / kept

Jack Nolan £1. 10. 6.
? Meeting Secs Board.

Letter to Joe Vize went today
Paddy.
Wrote Sid Jas B Copy kept in
pencil. £50 =

Diary, 24 April 1919

During 1919 and 1920 Collins quite frequently recorded the attendance at what appear to be meetings of his IRB circle. This is the only occasion on which he gives details of the circle's officers.

The diaries reflect a world of such subterfuges. Across 1919 there are at least nine references to the Wolfe Tone Memorial Committee, mostly to meetings: 'Meeting 9 41 W. T. Mem Cttee'.[12] The Wolfe Tone Memorial Committee emerged around 1898. Its unfulfilled public purpose was to promote the erection of a statue to Theobald Wolfe Tone at Stephen's Green while, more successfully, it organised pilgrimages to Bodenstown each June.[13] Critically, it 'was for a long time a public organisation through which the IRB worked'[14] and, after 1916, it was 'a cover for its revival'.[15] In September 1917, for instance, the committee organised the funeral of IRB president Thomas Ashe, claiming the costs from the INA&VDF, through Collins.[16] Later, on 19 April 1920, Collins wrote, 'Arranged tonight that £1000 handed over to WT Memorial Assn'.[17] Where he sourced the money, and to what purpose he handed it over, he did not say.

The Wolfe Tone Memorial Committee, and other IRB bodies, usually met at 41 Rutland (subsequently Parnell) Square, the Irish National Foresters' Hall. Collins's diary of 1918 records six different meetings there, and that of 1919 records sixteen. He met with groups but also individuals, for example on 6 January 1918 it was '12.30 at No. 41. Martin C.'[18] This was very likely Martin Conlon, centre of the Brothers Sheares Circle and member of the Supreme Council. Conlon would subsequently head up, for Collins, a unit charged with infiltrating trade unions.[19] A note in the diaries following a meeting at No. 41 on 14 June 1919 points toward its moment of origin and purpose: 'To work for the est of ITU & where IU are amlg to E Union to work for the breaking of the Amalgamation'.[20]

This development coincided, approximately, with Collins's transition from director of organisation to director of intelligence in the Irish Volunteers. Perhaps unsurprisingly, it is difficult to discern much that relates directly to the latter role. There are, for instance, references to Tom Cullen up to 23 January 1920 and after 12 November 1921, but not for the intervening period when he worked alongside Collins in the crucial role of assistant director of intelligence.[21]

The diaries are much more telling about Collins's time as director of organisation. In March 1918, in order to drive forward the revival of the Volunteers, a general headquarters (GHQ) staff was established with Richard Mulcahy as chief of staff.[22] Consequent to this, and the influx of new members due to the conscription crisis of April and May, there are signs of a changed pace. That spring and summer his diaries disclose contacts with fellow GHQ staff Mulcahy, Rory

O'Connor and Dick McKee,[23] a string of meetings at
McKee's Dublin Brigade HQ at 35 Lower Gardiner
Street,[24] and interactions with a series of men who
were, or would emerge as, key provincial leaders,
including Sean Treacy (Tipperary), Sean Boylan
(Meath), Paddy Colgan (Kildare), Eoin O'Duffy
(Monaghan), Sean O'Hegarty (Cork), Seamus Rafter
(Wexford) and Paddy Brennan (Clare).[25]

Eventually, inevitably, came the cost. Exactly
two months after his appearance in the diaries Rafter
died due to injuries sustained in an explosion.[26] Later,
in the spring of 1920, on the death of Tomás Mac
Curtain, Collins would measure that cost in funeral
wreaths—'Mary £2 for wreath' and 'Miss O'B also
wreath'—and a contribution to a new memorial
fund, for a new generation.[27]

Mary and Miss O'B are a reminder that
the revolutionary movement was more than a
brotherhood. The diaries contain one mention of
Cumann na mBan[28] but there are tens of references
to those like 'Miss Dooley New Ross' who delivered £100 for the Dáil loan.[29] His
diary of 1920 contains the addresses of several London-based women who were
supporters of the cause, including Gladys Hynes, an artist of Irish descent, and
Nellie Barrett, who would be jailed at Kilmainham during the Civil War, while
in that of 1919 Miss Killeen and Miss Barton are associated with what appear to
be a series of account numbers.[30]

On 24 April 1918, Kathleen Quinn embarrassed the authorities when
she succeeded in surreptitiously marrying Diarmuid Lynch, a member of the
supreme council of the IRB, while visiting him (with her sister and a priest) at
Dundalk prison. Lynch, who was under threat of deportation, had been refused
parole to marry.[31] This kind of stunt appealed to Collins and, five weeks later,
when Kathleen Lynch left Ireland, following her husband to America, Collins
made two entries: 'Saw Mrs Diarmuid Lynch last time. Sorry wish her luck' and
'Had a very nice note from Mrs D. L. She sailed on the Orduna this day.'[32]

The Fenian

Chiming with the times, the Queen's
theatre staged a production of
Hubert O'Grady's 'The Fenian', which
was first performed in 1889.

National Library of Ireland,
EPH E373

PLANETREE HOUSE,
DUCHESS OF BEDFORD'S WALK,
KENSINGTON, W. 8.
WESTERN 2671.

4th April 1964.

Dear Albert Fenton,

Your interesting letter has been forwarded to me and I feel it would not be an adequate response to simply autograph a card.

The future destiny of this very turbulent world in which we live rests mainly in the development of your generation. The evident fact that you have made a study of your country's recent past history is to me a heartening thought.

From time to time I am made aware of publications in Irish Newspapers which are biased or controversial in content when referring to political and military leaders of the era in which you appear to be interested.

I have read several of the books written about that period, and frankly I am disappointed. None have done justice to the people involved or the spirit which motivated them. Although not really good, the two most objective studies are "The Black and Tans" and "Bloody Sunday", but even these are full

---

Emmet Dalton to Albert Fenton, 4 April 1964

Emmet Dalton's letter, written to a young Albert Fenton, illustrates the loyalty and admiration that Collins inspired among many of those who worked with him.

Courtesy of Albert Fenton

of inaccuracies and mistakes, and both are written by Englishmen who have tried to be objective.

To have lived in those stirring times and to have had the privilege of close association with the volunteers in active service is a fond memory marred only by the tragedy of division caused by civil war. This is surely the greatest evil to befall any nation.

The most magnetic personality I have ever known was that which radiated from Michael Collins. To many he was a legend to some a myth, but to know him was to love him. Some intangible quality he possessed which could invoke service regardless of cost. He possessed all the virtues in great measure governed by a burning love of Ireland.

His desire to win freedom was such a driving force that he was intolerant of shortcomings in his less gifted associates, but he was quick to redress a wrong and very human in his understanding.

He died in my arms near his home. I loved him and revere his memory as Irelands architect of freedom

Sincerely,

Emmet Dalton

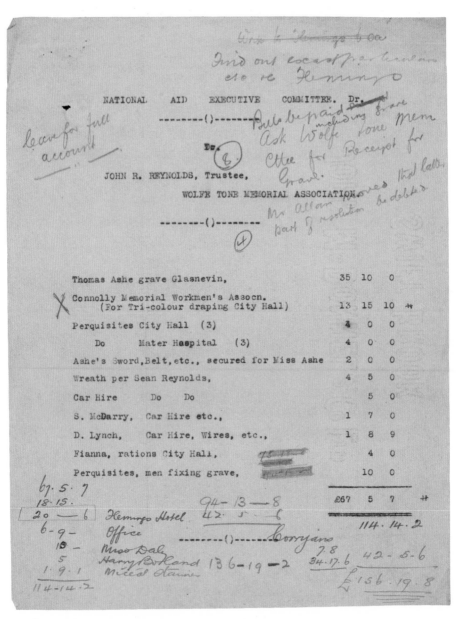

NATIONAL AID EXECUTIVE COMMITTEE. Dr.

--------()--------

Dr.

JOHN R. REYNOLDS, Trustee,

WOLFE TONE MEMORIAL ASSOCIATION

--------()--------

Thomas Ashe grave Glasnevin,	35	10	0
Connolly Memorial Workmen's Assocn. (For Tri-colour draping City Hall)	13	15	10
Perquisites City Hall (3)	4	0	0
Do Mater Hospital (3)	4	0	0
Ashe's Sword,Belt,etc., secured for Miss Ashe	2	0	0
Wreath per Sean Reynolds,	4	5	0
Car Hire Do Do		5	0
S. McDarry, Car Hire etc.,	1	7	0
D. Lynch, Car Hire, Wires, etc.,	1	8	9
Fianna, rations City Hall,		4	0
Perquisites, men fixing grave,		10	0
	£67	5	7

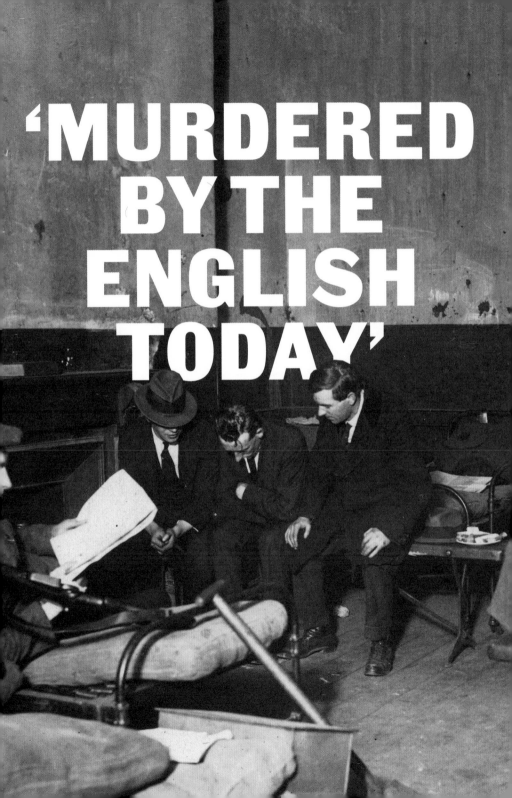

'MURDERED BY THE ENGLISH TODAY'

'MURDERED BY THE ENGLISH TODAY'

There came a point when keeping a diary was no longer wise.

By October 1920 Collins's quite diligent daily record had all but stopped.[1] November brought little more than solitary words, and the year ebbed out in repetition: 'away', 'away', 'away'.[2] It would be October 1921 before his diaries resumed.

All of which makes one entry in November 1920 stand more starkly out. After so many days of nothing, he wrote the emphatic: 'Dick McKee and Peadar Clancy were murdered by the English today'.[3] Murdered was not a word he had used before or would again and this was the only time he wrote in this way about 'the English', explicitly as an enemy. It was the diaries' sole, direct mention of violence; Collins dwelling on what was done and what was lost.

Pierce McCan succumbing to influenza was one of very few deaths he noted.[4] There was no mention of Seán Treacy's end, no word for Terence MacSwiney, although mass in Southwark Cathedral for MacSwiney's anniversary was on his list of appointments in London on 25 October 1921.[5] So, what set McKee and Clancy apart?

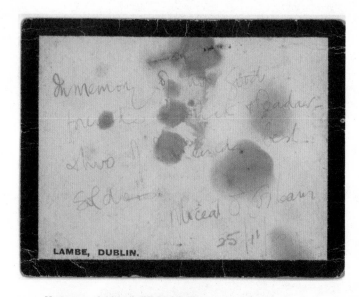

Mortuary card written by Michael Collins

Faded and weathered, this note was left by Collins on the grave of Dick McKee. It reads 'In memory of two Good friends – Dick & Peadar – two of Ireland's best Soldiers.'

At 9.00am on 21 November 1920 nineteen men were shot by the Dublin IRA. Fourteen of them died that day, a fifteenth perished later from his wounds. McKee as officer commanding the Dublin Brigade, Clancy as vice-brigadier, had been central to the planning of all that.[6] Retaliation followed at a match in Croke Park, where crown forces fired on the crowd, killing fourteen and injuring over sixty more. Captured on the night of 20–21 November, McKee and Clancy were beaten, interrogated and shot in Dublin Castle on the morning after this Bloody Sunday, allegedly trying to escape.[7] When Collins heard of their capture, he despaired, 'Good God. We're finished now. It's all up.'[8] McKee's loss was perhaps his biggest blow to date.

But McKee was more than that. Collins had known him since Frongoch.[9] Richard Mulcahy called their friendship 'one of the great companionships', and Collins's response suggests a deeply personal loss.[10] He helped to dress the bodies in Volunteer uniforms, maybe seeing for the first time the type of death that might befall him if caught.[11]

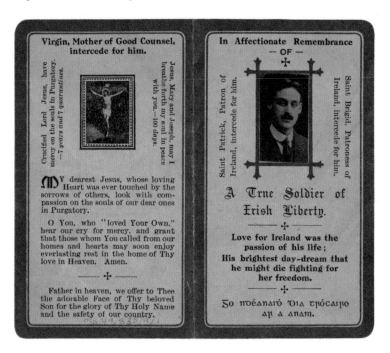

Memorial card for Dick McKee

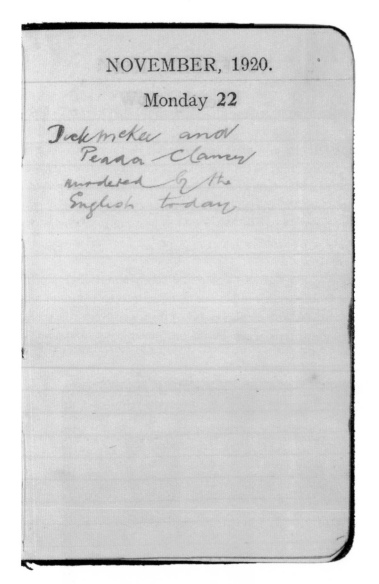

NOVEMBER, 1920.

Monday 22

Jack McKee and Peada Clancy murdered by the English today.

With thousands he went to Glasnevin to mark the first anniversary of McKee and Clancy's death, but his diary records meeting with McKee's mother alone.[12]

What he wrote in November 1920 suggests the rawness of his own loss; only the deaths of McKee and Clancy prompted him to write, not the fourteen in Croke Park.

↑
Diary, 22 November 1920

National Archives,
2021/110/3

→
A blank diary page, 1922

National Archives,
2021/110/5

KEEPING HIS SECRETS

KEEPING HIS SECRETS

Collins had his share of secrets to keep. He would have been a poor director of intelligence, a sorry president of the IRB, if he had not.

Clare Sheridan interviewed him in 1922 and described his life as 'a significant series of winks'.[1] Her readers, as so many since, were more charmed by a Collins spinning webs of intrigue than a minister for finance totting up the books. But his diaries are unlikely to solve the riddle of the man she described. In some ways, they make Collins, whether spymaster or bean-counter, that bit harder to reach.

Because some entries do seem to reflect the risks he ran, the 'Safe after night's work' of March 1919, the rather ominous 'Anything signed Michael Lalor will mean urgency...' of the following November, because his secrets weighed heavier as 1920 became 1921, it is tempting to read every entry as a key to his clandestine world.[2] The diary entries are short, often gnomic, and depending on the way we think of Collins, they suggest secrets in even the most ordinary things. In 'Saw Seamus etc.', 'Wrote to Johnny re Meeting etc', we might make a mystery out of an 'etc', read conspiracy into something commonplace, something dull.[3]

His rare use of Irish, his reference to 'Fear Eile', might well be weighted with special meaning, but might just as easily be a nickname, a bit of Irish no different from the odd 'Fuair buad' to record a match result, not so much a secret as a tokenistic thing.[4] For a man who did not doodle, are we to read more than the 'mood of a moment' into the underlining of a word, into the symbols that follow 'J.K. re D. + +'?[5] Maybe it was urgency more than secrecy, a simple prompt, a blunt reminder just to get work done. His best kept secret might be the ordinariness in it all.

On 9 September 1918 Collins wrote the words 'Particular day'.[6] Why that Monday merited such a description we may never know. Maybe it was about work, about a woman; maybe it meant less and less to him as the coming months confronted him with even more particular things.

In 'Particular day' Collins has given the curious a hare to chase, his 'rosebud' that someone will no doubt pick over and expose. But hopefully he gets to keep his one particular Monday, hopefully one secret stays known to him alone.

L.O.   No.579   28. 5. 21.

1/579   As I am writing away from back memos the number on this particular memo may not be correct. Perhaps it should be no. 578.

                           28. 5. 21.
2/579   I acknowledge receipt of nos. 1306, 1307, 1308, 1309, 1310. 1301 (dated 21st) 1312 (dated 22nd) 1313. 1314 (dated 23rd) 1315 dated 25th). All these came to hand on the 27th.

                           28. 5. 21.
3/579   . I am somewhat late in replying as the enemy brushed shoulders with me yesterday on Thursday and with my staff. They didn't get really very much, but they got a few things that I would much rather they had not got. They missed all my Staff also with the exception of one boy messenger. They just walked into the office where they expected to find me working. The information was good, and I ought to have been there at the time. It happened, however, that I was not. Neither was my Staff. It was the most providential escape yet. It will probably have the effect of making them think that I am even more mysterious than they believe me to be, and that is saying a good deal.

      Correspondence (1306)   28. 5. 21.
4/579   I note what you say. Your report on the question exactly deals with what I thought. I wonder if any arrangement like the following is possible ÷ Some place convenient to the station just to leave them, then about three reliable people to call on alternate nights . But no doubt this will have suggested itself to you and to A.M, so that it is not necessary that I should put it forward. If this arrangement is not possible, the only thing I can see for it is for me to leave it in your hands.

Michael Collins to Art O'Brien, 28 May 1921

Conscious of the dangers, Collins seems keenly
aware of the reputation he has acquired.

National Archives, DE/2/330/120

SUNDAY 8th.

M̶e̶e̶t̶:

MONDAY 9th.

Particula day.

White per Miss R.J

Diary, 9 September 1918

The meaning may well turn out to be obvious, but the 'mystery man of Ireland', as the *Manchester Guardian* once called him, maybe deserves to keep one day secret.

National Archives, 2021/110/1

TUESDAY 10th.

WEDNESDAY 11th.

Wrote.   stack.

"   Price

"   M. J Cronin Clonmel

15th Sunday after Trinity.

THURSDAY 12th.

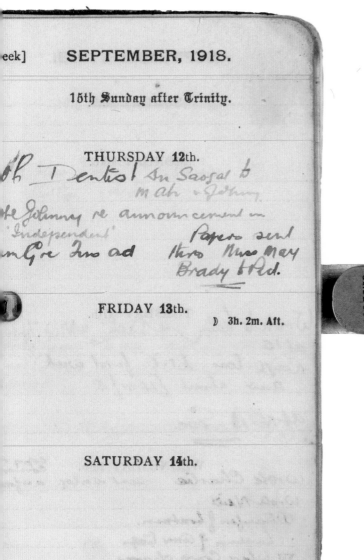

Oh. Dentist An Saogal to
M ah & Johnny

te Johnny re announcement in
'Independent'   Papers sent
mGre 2ns ad   thro Miss May
Brady & Red.

FRIDAY 13th.

☾ 3h. 2m. Aft.

SATURDAY 14th.

ML. COLLINS

CROOM 1922

↑
Collins at Croom, August 1922

Taken at Croom, Co. Limerick, not long before he died,
he seems here, at least, alone with his own thoughts.

National Library of Ireland, Ms 40,431/9

→
The interior of Lincoln Prison

Alamy Images

A
TAXI
FROM
LINCOLN

A TAXI FROM LINCOLN

On 4 February 1919 his diary reads: 'In todays [sic] papers—stop press in Dublin—there is a report that deV. escaped from Lincoln last night'.[1] One might almost believe it was news to him too. Of course, we know better. That adrenaline shout—'stop press in Dublin'—interrupting the matter-of-fact sentence carries more feeling. When you know, the whole entry winks: we did it.

Two weeks earlier, on 18 January, Collins recorded his leaving Dublin as 'Went for Holiday'.[2] Given that the first meeting of Dáil Éireann was fixed for three days later, it would have been a strange time to take a break. Instead, he travelled with Harry Boland to Manchester. From there, together with Liam McMahon and Paddy O'Donoghue, trusted local activists, and Frank Kelly who had journeyed ahead from Dublin to Lincoln, they plotted and reconnoitred.[3]

His diary entries for most of those days read like a businessman keeping track of his expenses: 'Taxi (2) £1 other fares lunch etc' and 'Taxi flat. Lunch 4. Incidentals. Small fares' though 'Taxi Lamp Muffler Fares Meals' is a little odder.[4] There was time for a trip to York on 22 January. Was this business or pleasure? We know from Paddy O'Donoghue that they made some time for the latter. He remembered that one evening, shortly before the escape, he brought Collins and Boland to a performance by Beecham's Opera Company. They had dinner afterward with Sir Thomas Beecham himself at the Midland Hotel: 'We were all naturally in very good form'.[5]

This must have been nothing as to their form when O'Donoghue, de Valera and his fellow escapees—Seán Milroy and Seán McGarry—pulled away in a taxi from Lincoln on the evening of 3 February. Because wartime fuel restrictions still pertained, they could not take a single taxi all the way to Manchester but set up a relay, switching cars at Worksop and then Sheffield.[6]

By 5 February Collins was back in the office with a better than usual holiday anecdote.[7] Michael Lynch remembered that, afterward, Collins liked to joke 'that the British taxi system must undoubtedly be one of the finest in the world'.[8]

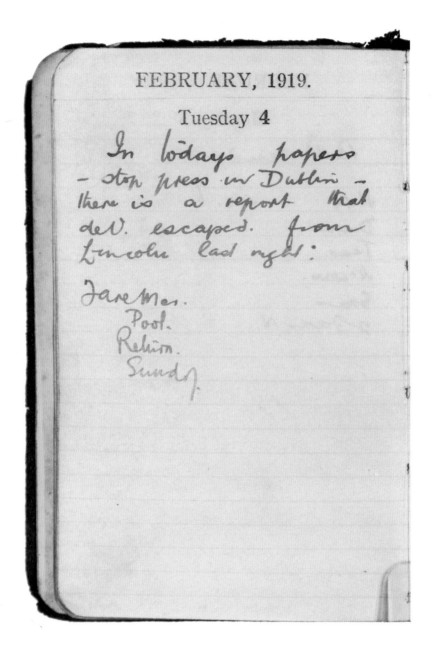

FEBRUARY, 1919.

Tuesday 4

In todays papers
- stop press in Dublin -
there is a report that
deV. escaped. from
Lincoln last night:

James.
Pool.
Return.
Sunday.

Diary, 4 February 1919

News of the escape did make it into the *Evening Herald* of 4 February.
In the days that followed, the press speculated as to how the
prisoners could have escaped and as to where they might be.

National Archives, 2021/110/2

↑
'Seán's Troubles'

When Seán McGarry hid a drawing of a prison key in plain sight in a Christmas cartoon home from Lincoln, he set in train the escape.

UCD Archives, P150/615

→
Republican prisoners, Cork, 1922

These prisoners were bound for internment.

National Library of Ireland, HOGW 11

PRISONERS

PRISONERS

Michael Collins's relationship to prisons changed in January 1922 when he became chairman of the Provisional Government. During the War of Independence, Dáil Éireann could claim an army, courts and (less convincingly) police, but the counter-state's attitude to prisons had remained just that, counter. As head of the new state's executive, however, Collins became responsible for a prison system that he had, till very recently, attacked.

At first the implications were pleasant enough. There were, for instance, releases to oversee. On 28 January Collins's diary lists three names followed by 'Borstal Institute Clonmel. Gen Dalton wrote on 24th'. Two of these were Joseph Dillon and Patrick Quane, who were seventeen and sixteen years-old on 28 April 1921, when sentenced to three years under the Restoration of Order in Ireland Act by a field general court martial at Limerick city. Their offence was larceny of a bicycle. When Dillon and Quane had 'commandeered' the bike from John McNamara, a messenger boy for an O'Connell Street chemist, they told him 'it was for the purposes of the I.R.A. under I.R.A. rules'. The borstal's register confirms that Dillon and Quane were released on 24 January 1922, 'by order of Government'.[1]

Con Shine, from Clarke's Bridge, Cork, was not so fortunate. While in that city on Friday 23 June, Collins did note, 'VII Con Shine Clonmel Prison'. Most likely one of Shine's relatives had pressed the eighteen year-old's case on the most powerful man in Ireland. But Shine was to remain a note not crossed through, one in a list of nine Collins made that day: a single task left unattended? What is certain is that no 'order of Government' arrived for Con Shine whose offences were shop-breaking and larceny.[2]

By then Collins had been campaigning for political prisoners for years. At first it was a job. In February 1917, Collins became paid secretary and general office manager of the INA&VDF. That organisation supported prisoners and their families from 32 Bachelor's Walk, Dublin, and on Saturday, 5 January 1918, we find in the diaries a first '3OC at 32'.[3] From then, till Collins's arrest on 2 April,[4] signposts to such meetings are a regular feature.[5] After April there is just one, 4 May, and none once he left the INA&VDF's employ in early July.[6]

very truth an evening for the open road. By standing on my table I can see Knocknarea in the distance or actually close at hand. It is at present bathed in the light of the sinking sun and the cairn over the resting place of Maeb the warrior is scarcely discernible. Oh! Lord the unrest of soul. There is never a moment during the day that I cannot make use of a light word or pretend to a visitor that I am perfectly at ease & content. Now here alone I am in a state of appalling loneliness with the blackest despair in my heart. Of course the reason for my sadness & loneliness is the thought of the work I might be doing. Instead I am forcibly kept idle and inactive. Even ones mind seems to grow sterile in captivity. An hour of application when one is free is worth a days work in jail.

Judging by the papers today the English ministers were in rampant mood last night in St Stephens over Conscription for Ireland. They simply spat Compulsory Service at the occupants of the Irish Benches. I do not envy those occupants their feelings now. It is interesting to note en passant that Harbison the recently elected member for East Tyrone said if there were another

---

Account in Michael Collins's hand of his detention in Sligo Gaol

As the diary of his time in Sligo Gaol reveals, the sociable workaholic Collins found imprisonment a terrible strain.

National Library of Ireland, Ms 49,667/1

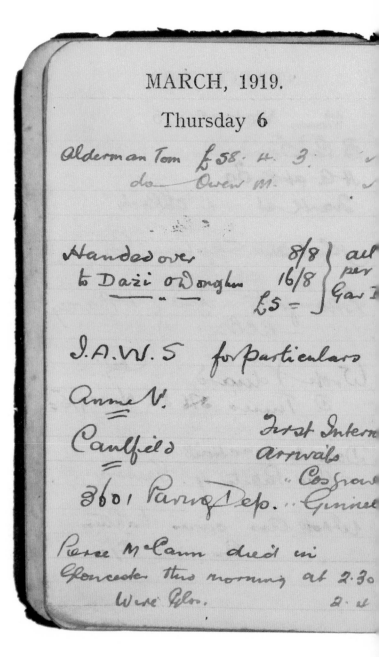

MARCH, 1919.

Thursday 6

Alderman Tom £58. 4. 3.
do Owen M.

Handed over 8/8 } all
to Dazi o'Donghu 16/8 } per
£5 = } Gav I

I.A.W.S for particulars

Anne V.

Caulfield   First Intern
                             arrivals
                                  "Cosgrave
3601 ParneDep. ...Guinne

Pierce McCann died in
Gloucester this morning at 2.30
Were Glos.   2. ul

Friday 7

6.30 Noll =

Wrote Willie C.
. Pat m cDes.

Directory =

Wrote Austin & Saman.

Maryboro Diarmuid

Wires etc   4.6
do m.e.   1.2
Car   3.6

Jim Falon   2 =

к Danff.   VI re Pres Wilson ⎫
Alvoeshes.   VII re Ned B   ⎬ 8/3/19
Case   IX re Pastoral . ⎭
Fitzgerald

When 'arrested O'Connell bdge by O'Brien and Bruton' that April, Collins began what was his second period of imprisonment.[7] He kept a separate, more reflective account or diary of the next twenty days. Of 18 April in Sligo Gaol he wrote:

> Mrs Hanley was to visit me again today. She has been most awfully kind and thoughtful. Really its [sic] hard not to feel embarrassed when I think of all the trouble and inconvenience I am putting people to. Especially as when at large myself I am the most thoughtless person in every way in the world. There is indeed plenty of cause for my being ashamed.[8]

The evidence, including that of his regular pocket diaries, suggests he was hard on himself. Prisoners were often on his mind, albeit for a complex set of reasons. His own experiences had heightened his empathy for, and sense of duty to, those incarcerated, or at least some of them. For a time too it was a matter of professional pride and, though certain that his own days in prison were wasted, Collins understood the power of political prisoners. He knew of the trouble they could cause, that they possessed the capacity to rend hearts, and that an escape was a coup.

We've long known, through collections of surviving correspondence, that Collins maintained regular contact with Austin Stack while the latter led Irish Volunteer prisoners at Belfast and, subsequently, at Strangeways, Manchester, during 1918 and 1919. The diaries do more than confirm this. 'Wrote Austin', or variations of that phrase, constitute a refrain from July 1918 through to August 1919. They consulted in early November 1918 when the prisoners at Belfast were deciding whether to participate in an official inquiry, chaired by Justice William Dodd, into alleged brutalities that had taken place there during a June protest. He 'Wrote Austin (1) Enquiry . . .' and 'Stack re Gavan D[uffy] and Enquiry', while in April 1919 he 'Sent Aus Dodd Report' on its coming out.[9] On St Patrick's Day 1919 the entry 'Aus'[10] corresponds to a letter in which he provided Stack with news of Dublin Corporation's support for a campaign of disobedience then ongoing at Belfast and of the escape from Mountjoy the night before of Robert Barton: 'Its [sic] only a faggot to keep the pot boiling'.[11] According to Barton, 'Mick Collins was in a street near by waiting to congratulate me.'[12] It is surely not too far a stretch to suggest that this was the cryptic 'Tonight's appointment' in Collins's diary.[13]

Photograph with Constance Markievicz (centre), 15 March 1919

Pictured here at Liberty Hall after her release, since May of the previous year Constance Markievicz had been held at Holloway prison with Kathleen Clarke and, for a time, Hannah Sheehy Skeffington.

In that letter of 17 March Collins also mentioned his concerns for some of the 'German Plot' prisoners, recently released from England: 'A few of the men who returned are very poorly – particularly Paidín O'Keeffe.'[14] Over the preceding fortnight he had counted them home in his diaries, alive and dead: 'First Internee Arrivals Cosgrave Ginnell';[15] 'Mrs Clarke';[16] 'Countess arrived in Ath Cliath';[17] and more sombrely, 'Pierce McCann died in Gloucester this morning at 2.30'[18] followed by 'P. McCan remains arrived Dunleary. Left K.bridge 1 O'Clock'.[19]

The INA&VDF had been succeeded by a prisoner support organisation that wore its politics more overtly, the Irish Republican Prisoners' Dependents Fund (IRPDF).[20] Collins served on the committee and, occasionally, across 1919 he noted in his diaries its meetings or donations handed to him as he went about his work.[21] Mountjoy featured in mundane ways on mundane days, 'Cigarets [sic] for Joy' on 24 November 1919, and in significant ways on significant days: 'Releases from Joy today' on 14 April 1920.[22] Later, in London in 1921, he used

17 3. 19

A' a Caog

There must be a letter of mine you
haven't got. A letter I wrote on the 11th acknowledging
yours. The note to Joe McE puzzles me though as
I do not remember that. But yours to H and
yours to me (5th) were duly received. Perhaps
by this time you'll have got mine of the 11th
which will set your mind at rest.

The Corporation were as you may
imagine rushed into the business. Now that
they have gone so far I'll keep at the
Lord Larry. As soon as they did I - by
the way - doubts were raised as to the
truth of the statements. I am sorry there was
some exaggeration but it couldn't be
helped and you'll see from the enclosed
rough ~~written~~ draft that the written
word was not ~~even~~ overstating the case.

How I do hope you'll be released.
The Internment Camp in my opinion - except
for the immediate relief 'twould give — is not
any use. No precedent would be established
and we must make up our minds
that each new group going to jail
will have to fight its ~~own~~ own case.
They'll never be faithful to any agreement

Michael Collins to Austin Stack, 17 March 1919

The correspondence between Collins and Austin Stack, dating from the latter's periods
of imprisonment, suggest that they worked closely and effectively during 1918 and
1919. Later, their relationship would sour. Collins refers to this letter in his diary.

But I need not dilate on this point to
you. It would be presumption. Although
I've not mentioned your opinion about
release to anyone — (I dislike - as much as
you do being the means of spreading
rumors and raising false hopes) I feel
its fairly likely and will be anxiously
awaiting its consummation.

Last night there was another rescue
escape, release. Anything you like. R.C.
Barton is free anyway. Its only a
faggot to keep the pot boiling.

I am sending you a copy of the Óglác.
The job is getting increasingly difficult and
to add to it I believe they're on my track
again. I'm sick of it — but as Tone says "It is
in vain" etc.

A few of the men who returned are
very poorly — particularly Paidin O'Keeffe. He
looks very downcast and his "giz" seems
vanished. However we hope he'll pull up. Eamon
Bulfin is not yet free. I fear its looks like
Deportation. No more at the moment. I'm not
feeling in any kind of form & this is a sorry
production consequently. Have you changed your
mind about that other job yet .?

With every good wish.

M.

A scenes outside Mountjoy during a hunger strike

During hunger strikes and executions Mountjoy prison became a focus of vigil and protest. The large intimidating crowds imposed upon the prison and the atmosphere in the city.

RTÉ Archives, 0505/033

the meetings of the Committee on the Observance of the Truce to press the case of prisoners and internees.[23] Reflecting this, his diaries referred to conditions at, or reports on, Wormwood Scrubs prison, and Spike and Rath camps.[24] During those busy days he attended to individual cases too, including that of Pat Harte who had been transferred from prison to Broadmoor Criminal Lunatic Asylum and 'Sean O'Connor Rath Intern Camp mother dying'.[25]

How strange it must have been then, on 7 July 1922, when he found himself considering 'Question of Prisoners & release on guarantees' and a 'Note re Kilmainham & readiness'.[26] Ignoring Con Shine can hardly have prepared him for that day. Yet, if the Provisional Government was to create its Irish Free State, to establish a monopoly of violence in the face of republican resistance, then Michael Collins faced becoming a gaoler on a mass scale. And so, as Paidín O'Keeffe became deputy military governor of Mountjoy that July, Collins's days filled with 'Prison Accommodation between 8 & 9', 'Note re Prison Accom. M.boro. Kilkenny. Dundalk' and

> III Galway Jail,
> III(a)Sligo [Jail]
> IV Waterford [Jail][27]

→
Two women walking by Johnson's jewellers, Grafton Street, Dublin

Collins bought a watch for Kitty Kiernan in Johnson's jewellers. He made a note to pay the balance of the cost on 23 December 1921. Johnson's had made a brooch for Queen Victoria, a coronet for the Countess of Granard, and the Liam MacCarthy Cup.

National Library of Ireland, CLAR9

PRIVATE
LIVES

PRIVATE LIVES

Before Kitty there was Helen.

On 10 May 1919 Collins's confided to his diary 'Wrote to Miss Helen K. asking for my written matter'.[1] Helen Kieran didn't want him, and a spurned Michael Collins wanted his letters back. The woman who had prompted him to contemplate 'Birds singing and chirping', 'Beautiful sunshine', the wonders of 'a most glorious April evening' when she visited him in Sligo Gaol in April 1918, had chosen a solicitor over Michael Collins, and if we are to believe Frank O'Connor, Helen Kiernan, 'the Parisian Rose', broke Michael Collins's heart.[2] If she did, then this request for his 'written matter' is the only hint his diaries give of this hurt. In his diaries, at least, Collins was scrupulously discreet about his private life.

This is not to imply his diaries are empty of possibility or opportunity. For those who wish to believe he pursued passionate affairs, particularly during his time at the Treaty negotiations in London, his diary entries about phone calls and meetings with Moya Llewelyn Davies and Lady Hazel Lavery, the two women he has been linked to most, are so brief as to be interpreted in any number of ways.[3] When in London he did phone Moya Llewelyn Davies, met her on 1 December 1921, 'Moya 3.30 to 3.45'.[4] There are mentions of Lady Lavery, but almost as many of her husband, Sir John.[5] Whether Collins was, as George Bernard Shaw put it, her 'Sunday husband', the diaries neither confirm nor deny.[6] Entries such as 'Lady Lavery & New books Etc.' might suggest a shared passion for fiction as much as each other.[7] But the diaries, for all their mentions of 'Lady L' and 'M.L.D', in their own quiet ways kept coming back to Kitty.[8]

They tell us when, if not always when, 'I was at Granard' visiting Kitty Kiernan, but they leave it to other sources and perhaps a prurient imagination to conceive of what went on there.[9] The diaries are sober companions to his fitfully passionate letters sent to 'Dearest Kit', 'Kitty darling', 'Kit, Kit, I wish you were with me now'.[10] But they tell of the more mundane things couples do for each other, the quieter, less dramatic acts, the obligations that come with affection. Collecting parcels for her, paying the balance on the gold watch he bought for her, returning it to 'Johnstons' [sic] jewellers to get it mended or changed.[11] He bought her 'swede' [sic] gloves.[12] He reminded himself to buy tickets for La Scala for when she came to Dublin, and made an appointment with Dr Robert Farnan

Kitty Kiernan

Alamy Stock Photo

for her.[13] Farnan was a gynaecologist, but Collins also sent IRA men to see him when they suffered from 'weak nerves' after what they had seen and done.[14] He wrote a note of introduction for her to Farnan: 'She says probably unjustly that there is something wrong with her. I wonder if you'd mind seeing and advising.'[15] '[Y]ou see I have begun taking real care of you', he wrote to Kitty.[16] At 31 and 29, these were two mature people getting ready for married life.

The gloves, the watch, the getting and remembering for Kitty, it was all at a prosaic remove from the younger, more carefree, more melodramatic Collins of New Year's Day 1919. 'Saw Lady today <u>for last</u> time' suggests a rather grand passion had come to a very final end.[17] Whether reciprocated or unrequited it is impossible to tell; the 'Lady' is known to Collins alone.

I
Boland & yourself
are the chief nominations
for HonSecs. Is says he
wont run against the
fear I am of opinion that
Proposal in Dulcan
be ought
7/10/18 what do you
think?

asob₁f em a and

I have just got your kind
message per Miss O'Brien — not Angela—
and am writing a note to
reassure you about the lady of my
affections. So far as I am concerned
I am satisfied I have very good
reason to be. At the same time I
think I know the story you have
heard. There is I am convinced
nothing in it. Of course like
all such things there is an
element of risk which must be
taken. You may I think rely
on me to be careful enough. If
there is a Mrs C I know all
about the story. They should not

MS 5848/11 (1)

Michael Collins to Austin Stack, 7 October 1918

Here he writes of 'the lady of my affections' and of gossip Stack might have heard. Is the mentioned 'Grace' the 'Lady'?

National Library of Ireland, Ms 5,848/11

be worrying you with such things!
Perhaps you would be able to
let me know what you heard.
On the other hand perhaps I
have got hold of the wrong end
of the stick & that its Graces own
family you are suspicious of.
      Peace. What is your Opinion.
Generally speaking Im not very
impressed. It must come sometime
thó some of the greatest signs is
the newspaper offensive waged by
the British Press for some time
back. Its very hard to form
an opinion that one could
stand up to as we only
get such garbled versions.
Take Bulgaria for instance. I

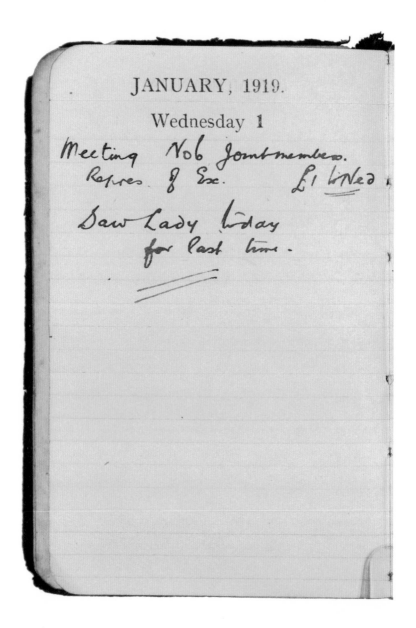

JANUARY, 1919.

Wednesday 1

Meeting Nob Joint members.
Repres. of Exc.   £1 to Ned

Saw Lady today
for last time.

THE
GAA

THE GAA

On Sunday, 6 April 1919, according to his diary, Michael Collins met 'Luke' at 12.30.[1] It seems likely that this was Luke O'Toole, secretary of the Gaelic Athletic Association (GAA), because Collins had reason to be grateful to O'Toole that lunchtime.[2]

The day before, at Croke Park, the footballers of Wexford played Tipperary, a team they had defeated seven weeks earlier when winning the All-Ireland title of 1918; Wexford's fourth in-a-row. The papers billed this renewed contest between the best teams in Ireland the 'De Valera Cup'.[3]

Éamon de Valera was then at the peak of his popularity. Ten days before, he was expected to attend a civic reception to celebrate his escape from Lincoln prison. But, when the authorities banned the event Sinn Féin cancelled it, at de Valera's urging and despite Collins's protests.[4] This time, just four days after his election as president of Dáil Éireann, de Valera turned up. When he threw the ball in, he was both taunting the authorities and raising money for the Irish Republican Prisoners' Dependents' Fund. With the ceremonies complete, and to the cheers of around 25,000, de Valera joined Collins on the side-line, leaving Harry Boland to referee the match.[5] O'Toole, meanwhile, counted the IRPDF's takings.

At some point over that weekend Collins recorded the gate, £1085, while underneath he jotted down the result, 'W. 2pts Tipp one': political activist and football fan by turn.[6] Collins regularly mixed revolution and pleasure in this manner. Two months earlier, on 9 February, he noted, and almost certainly attended, a hurling match between Dublin (the All-Ireland champions of 1917) and Limerick (the reigning champions) in what the papers described as the final of the National Aid Tournament.[7] It garnered one last pot for the INA&VDF, which was then in the process of winding up its activities.[8]

Earlier again, on Monday, 5 August 1918, Collins described himself as 'not very wel (sic)'.[9] It was the morning after the day before, now known as 'Gaelic Sunday': Collins, it seems, enjoyed it. On 'Gaelic Sunday' the GAA organised matches across Ireland in a successful mass protest against the government's attempt to force the association to apply for a permit for each game they fixed.

Two weeks later, on 18 August, the man who used his position as secretary of the Ulster Council of the GAA to drive Gaelic Sunday, Eoin O'Duffy, made his first appearance in Collins's diaries.[10] O'Duffy is one of several to feature regularly

Arthur Griffith, Eamon de Valera, Laurence O'Neill and Michael Collins

Enjoying the occasion that was the de Valera Cup.

Courtesy of GAA Museum and Archive, Croke Park

who were both revolutionary colleagues and GAA officials: 'PS' [O'Hegarty],[11] JJW[alsh],[12] 'SAM' [Maguire],[13] Chris[topher M.] Byrne,[14] the 'Aus' or 'Austin' of countless occasions during 1918 and 1919 reduced to a single 'Stack' by 1921,[15] and 'Harry' in 1918 and 1919 who became 'Boland' in 1922.[16] Is it too simple to suggest that Collins's interest in a Dublin hurling league final between Collegians and Faughs, played in February 1919, rested on the fact that Boland played?[17] Either way, sporting talk surely eased the friendships Collins built with these men, those that lasted and those that did not.

And Collins was interested. His GAA was not all networks and ulterior motives. In London, a decade earlier, the Geraldines club had been a home away from home, while in 1919 he followed the All-Ireland football championship closely. Into his diary went the drawn semi-final between Kerry and Galway (24 August), Dublin's defeat of the champions Wexford (31 August), their subsequent

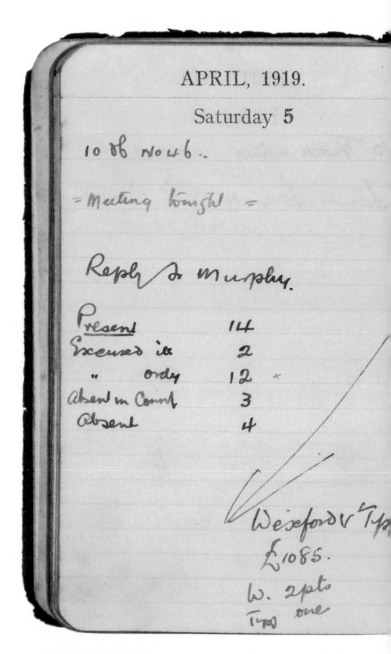

APRIL, 1919.

Saturday 5

10 of No 46 ..

= Meeting tonight =

Reply to Murphy.

Present	14
Excused ill	2
" ordy	12
Absent in Conft	3
Absent	4

Wexford v Typ
£1085.
W. 2 pts
Typ one

Diary, 5–6 April 1919

Collins records the takings from, and the score of, the de Valera Cup.

5th in Lent. **Sunday 6**

1 O'clock at 46   Diarmind

12.30 do   - 41   Luke

Easter with drawn £41. 13. 4

Kitly about 4.30

Roll   19   Luke
Present   16
Ex cur.   1   Shannon. ✓
Abs   2   Note O'Boa. ✓

Sub   20/6
arrears 5/6   15   Board 12/1.

Diarmind

Roll. 34
Present 18.
ce   12
Abs.   7   Donal O'Connor
Subc.   23/=   Board · 18/2

←
Dan Fraher

Dan Fraher, from Dungarvan, was another contact of Collins who combined the GAA and revolution. A champion athlete in the 1880s, he became president of a revived GAA Waterford County Board in 1901 and the first treasurer of the association's Munster Council (1901–12). He was also president of the Gaelic League in Dungarvan. His name appears six times in Collins's diaries between April and July 1919, passing on significant sums of money from west Waterford. Though by then elderly, his activities would see him interned at Ballykinlar camp in 1920 and 1921.

Waterford County Museum, Dungarvan, EK1687

defeat to Kildare (7 September) and Kildare's ultimate triumph over Galway (28 September).[18] Maybe it was a sense of new beginnings let loose by the end of Wexford's imperial phase that caught Collins's attention that autumn, perhaps it was the emergence of a new hero, Kildare's Larry Stanley.[19] Though it is doubtful that Collins attended all of these games, for a couple of months at least, keeping up mattered. Then, as happens, he turned to other things.

→
Michael Collins with briefcase

This photograph is held with the files of the Dáil loan. It represents Collins as a vigorous, busy minister for finance.

National Archives, DE/2/530

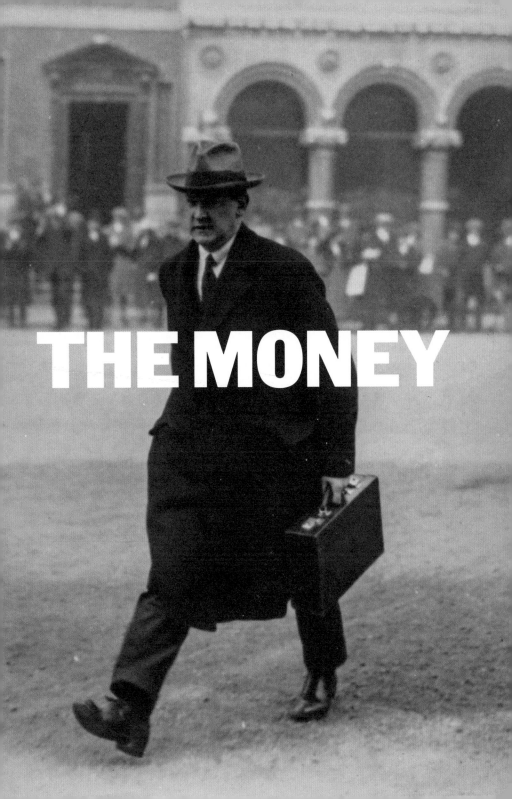

THE MONEY

Michael Collins spent a lot of time thinking about money. If we were to mistake these diaries for a straightforward map of his mind, then we might come to believe that for the first six months of 1920, he thought about little else. That his every waking hour filled with money, day after day, in long lists, representing amounts to be lodged and acknowledged. It is important not to exaggerate nor to lose perspective, and yet the diaries reveal patterns, throwing his working life into relief. Just as they tell us that re-organising the Irish Volunteers was a priority for him in the summer of 1918, they confirm, in £s and figures, that the money, the money, the money possessed him for long stretches of 1920.

Collins's relationship to the money, to the accumulation and use of it for revolutionary purposes, had been building over several years. At first, we tend to find it encompassed in the word 'fund'. Before the diaries, there was the Irish National Aid & Volunteer Dependents' Fund. Then came the Irish Republican Prisoners' Dependents' Fund, which keeps bobbing to the surface throughout: 'Seumas Hughes re RPD Fund', 'Meeting R.P.D Fund', '3/6 to prisoners' fund' and '£5 Prisoner Fund' are just a few examples from 1919.[1]

That year too, on 19 May, in his role as adjutant-general of the Irish Volunteers, Collins wrote to Art O'Brien in London, explaining that the headquarters staff had decided to 're-institute the Defence of Ireland Fund' with a 'huge <u>Drawing of Prizes</u>'. He sent on 100 books of raffle tickets for sale, setting out his expectations: 'As the Irish abroad cannot take so active a part in Volunteer work as those at home, we confidently expect a vigorous effort in the one way they can be equally useful – the supplying of Funds.'[2] The diaries suggest that Collins had embarked on a round of arm-twisting. On 6 May, he 'Wrote Woods' about 'Tickets Drawing Prizes', on 8 May he 'Wrote Neill re drawing tickets' and on 15 May it was the turn of 'Joe today c[arbon] c[opy] kept (tickets)'.[3]

By then he had been collecting for another, more substantial, fund for several months. Dáil Éireann called it the Self-Determination Fund (SDF), having improvised it in the early weeks of 1919 as a method of gathering into their new and bare coffers money collected during 1918 for the now redundant Anti-Conscription Fund.[4] The money in the Anti-Conscription Fund was due for return to the subscribers, but Dáil Éireann asked them to pass it on to the new cause. At first, this happened in dribs and drabs. For instance, Collins noted in his diary on 27 March, '9/= from Fr Bowden to N[ational] Self D Fund'.[5]

Anti-Conscription Fund Distribution.

The Anti-Conscription Fund will be Distributed in this Parish commencing on

SUNDAY, 27th APRIL, 1919.

Which Nation are you going to Support—
IRELAND or ENGLAND ?
You can back your own Nation and Support your Delegates in Paris by handing your Subscription back to the Self Determination Fund.
ENGLAND is Spending MILLIONS to Defeat YOU.
Are YOU going to Stand for Ireland in this her Hour of Need ?
Your Subscription will speak for YOU ! Hand it over—'Tis Now or Never !
The Irish in America stand solid, their Delegates are in Paris on YOUR behalf. The Irish at home must inspire them.
Don't play England's Game !

EIRE ABU.

"GAZETTE," PRINTERS. ARMAGH

Collins assumed ultimate responsibility for all of this when he became minister for finance on 2 April 1919. Immediately, that familiar hectoring energy became apparent with a decision to focus minds through a national 'distribution', beginning on 27 April. This was backed by propaganda that urged subscribers to support 'Ireland' by 'handing Your subscription back': 'Your Subscription will speak for YOU! Hand it over – 'Tis Now or Never!'[6] The initiative was reflected in Collins's diary with 'notices for transfer tomorrow's Ard Comhairle'.[7] In the weeks that followed, *Nationality* sought to add momentum to the collective transfer by publishing lists of those towns and parishes where this was agreed.[8] The SDF

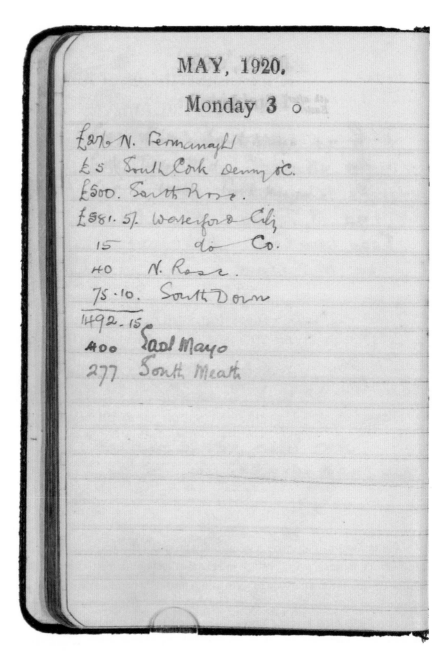

MAY, 1920.

Monday 3

£276 N. Fermanagh
£5 South Cork Denny &c.
£500. South Rose.
£581. 5/. Waterford City
15 do Co.
40 N. Rose.
75.10. South Down
————————
1492.15
400 Earl Mayo
277 South Meath

D A I L   E I R E A N N   L O A N.

NETT AMOUNTS RECEIVED AT HEAD OFFICE AS ON THE 27th. SEPTR. 1920.

CONNACHT

GALWAY:	Connemara	1564:13:4
	East	4588: 0:0
	North	3019: 5:0
	South	3295:10:0
LEITRIM:		5087: 7:2
MAYO:	East	3613:10:0
	North	4021: 5:0
	South	7087: 0:0
	West	5073: 0:0
ROSCOMMON:	North	4806: 0:0
	South	4867: 0:0
SLIGO:	North	3675: 0:0
	South	3709: 9:6

TOTAL: £57,977: 0:0

MUNSTER

CLARE:	East	13616:14:6
	West	7713: 0:0
CORK:	City	12067: 0:0
	East	6534:15:0
	Mid	7237: 2:6
	North	6497: 0:0
	North East	3787:10:0
	South	4876:15:10
	South East	2085: 0:0
	West	4350: 0:0
KERRY	East	5154:10:0
	North	9229: 0:0
	South	3104: 2:0
	West	8571:15:0
LIMERICK:	City	5991: 0:0
	East	32285: 0:0
	West	17385: 0:0
TIPPERARY:	East	4864:10:0
	Mid	2951: 6:6
	North	4377: 0:0
	South	4458: 0:0
WATERFORD:	City	636: 5:0
	County	4550: 0:0

TOTAL : £172,533: 6:4

LEINSTER

CARLOW:		3383: 5:0
DUBLIN:	Clontarf	2204:10:0
	College Gn	2101: 5:0
	Harbour	1058:15:0
	Pembroke	2580: 0:0
	Rathmines	1235: 0:0
	St.James'	1455: 0:0
	St.Michans	2781:15:0
	St.Stephens	2322:10:0
	St.Patricks	2161:10:0
	North Co.	1370: 5:0
	South Co.	2125:10:0
KILDARE:	North	2381:10:0
	South	3445: 0:0
KILKENNY:	North	2912: 0:0
	South	5281:10:0
LONGFORD:		5802: 0:0
LOUTH:		2575: 5:0
MEATH:	North	1902: 4:0
	South	2262: 0:0
OFFALY:		9198: 1:6
LEIX & OSSORY		10930:12:6
WESTMEATH:		4660: 0:0
WEXFORD:	North	3280:10:0
	South	4457: 0:0
WICKLOW:	East	819: 4:6
	West	3713: 0:0

TOTAL: £87,499: 2:6

ULSTER

ANTRIM:	Belfast	2355: 6:6
	East & Nth	196: 0:0
	Mid	152: 0:0
	South	427: 0:0
ARMAGH:	Mid	527:10:0
	North	322:10:0
	South	1665: 0:0
CAVAN:	East	4227: 4:5
	West	3211: 5:0
DERRY:	City	1376: 0:0
	North	772:10:0
	South	713: 0:0
DONEGAL:	East	1032: 0:0
	North	885: 0:0
	South	1333:10:0
	West	675: 0:0
DOWN:	East & Mid	2672: 0:0
	South	1845:10:0
	West	199: 0:0
FERMANAGH:	North	1768: 0:0
	South	1488: 0:0
MONAGHAN:	North	2457:18:0
	South	5706: 0:0
TYRONE:	North East	2307:10:0
	North West	1466:10:0
	South	1551: 0:0

TOTAL : £41,319: 4:2

GRAND TOTALS.

CONNACHT	57,977: 0:0
LEINSTER	87,499: 2:6
MUNSTER	172,533: 6:4
ULSTER	41,319: 4:2
CUMANN NA mBAN	801: 0:0
BRITAIN & FRANCE	11,719: 8:0
	£371,849: 1:0

Subscriptions by constituency to the Dáil Éireann Loan, September 1920

Collins and his staff kept meticulous track of subscriptions to the Dáil loan.

National Library of Ireland, ILB 300 p 2 [Item 46]

proved the Dáil's most important source of income till the autumn of 1919, bringing in £42,054 up to 31 October, while smaller amounts kept trickling in during 1920.[9]

On 9 May 1919 Collins recorded, 'Meeting Dail [sic] today Made Ministerial Statement on Finance'.[10] It was his first, and worth noting. The speech was a lengthy indictment of the economic exploitation and over-taxation of Ireland since the Act of Union.[11] Most of the time though, he looked forward, in particular to his key fund-raising scheme, usually known as the Dáil Loan. Launched in the autumn, this offered bonds for sale (from £1 to £100) with the aim of raising £250,000 in Ireland. Overall, it was an enormous success, if more so in some places than in others.[12]

The beginnings were modest—on 25 October, the diaries indicate, Collins wrote to John Reynolds with three certs for named subscribers, one share each—but gradually the diaries become a daily accounting of sums, both considerable and modest, from various places.[13] The constituency of Mid-Cork was one of the success stories, built systematically village by town. On 2 February 1920 '(a) Ballincollig (b) Inchigeela & Macroom' feature in the diary, mirroring a letter of acknowledgement from Collins to Terence MacSwiney. Next day, Collins noted money from Millstreet: and, again, the letter went out to MacSwiney.[14]

It kept coming, including '£100 Gold West Cork',[15] and he kept counting, passing it on 'to D.O'D'.[16] Daithí O'Donoghue was, as Patrick O'Sullivan Greene has explained, a crucial figure at the Department of Finance, 'who opened the bank accounts, made the payments and moved the money'.[17] Keeping the money safe for Michael Collins.

CLERGY

CLERGY

On 18 May 1920 Collins created one more list, eleven places and eleven sums of money. In a few cases, he noted down a name. One reads, 'Galway N[orth] 260 Fr Tom Burke.'[1]

Galway North and Burke had many parallels. On 24 June Collins wrote, 'Roscommon N[orth] £830 per Fr Glynn Drumlion', and further down that page, 'Tyrone South Dungannon 195 Per Fr Maguire'. The next day it was '£26.7.6 per Rev Canon Doyle', followed by 'Clare East 255.10 Suspense per Fr O'Kennedy', and 'Cavan East 268. 10 Fr O'Connell'. On 12 May it had been '£1024 West Mayo Fr Conry' while months earlier, on 17 January, Collins rewarded the spectacular with a verb, albeit one that qualified the priest's achievement: '£9489 passed on from Fr Hayes W[est] L[imeri]ck'. More modest, but not forgotten, was '£6 Westmeath Fr Keappock'. And just in case you think we are bluffing, we offer up 'Fr Keane N. Rosc[ommon] Clonquin 152' and '46 10/= Rev Fr Malachy Brennan'. [2]

The cash was coming in and, to an extent that might surprise some, the Catholic clergy was a conduit. On reflection, this is not so strange. In January 1920, priests held the office of president on 24 of Sinn Féin's 87 constituency executives (comhairle ceanntair).[3] As Brian Heffernan has put it, the 'Sinn Féin priest was a very common phenomenon' though he illustrated the divisions that existed among the clergy by quoting J.P. Conry (he of '£1024 West Mayo'). In August 1919, Conry wrote to John Hagan, vice-rector of the Irish College in Rome, that he was 'astonished at the number priests I meet who do not think our way. So many of them are in the old groove. These,' he continued, 'simply laugh at us.'[4]

For the particular priests who appear in the diary being a bagman for Michael Collins was often but one measure of their radical nationalism. Tom Keane, Thomas Maguire and Malachy Brennan—curates in Killina in Roscommon, Clogher in Tyrone, and Ballinasloe in Galway respectively—were all presidents of their local comhairle ceanntair.[5] While Patrick O'Connell, parish priest at Cootehill, was a prominent supporter of Arthur Griffith during the East Cavan by-election of 1918.[6]

As early as May 1916, General John Maxwell had complained to the Bishop of Limerick, Edward O'Dwyer, that Michael Hayes was 'a dangerous menace to the peace and safety of the Realm'. In November 1920, the police would raid the curates' residence in which Hayes lived in Newcastle West.[7] A month earlier, in October 1920, J. Glynn, along with another priest, James Roddy, was arrested at, and convicted of participating in, a banned meeting.[8] The authorities did not imprison them but they did send William O'Kennedy, president of St Flannan's College, Ennis, to Bere Island internment camp. The crown forces arrested him when, in early July 1921, they raided the annual retreat of the diocese of Killaloe, an event presided over by Bishop Michael Fogarty, an ally of Collins and a trustee of the Dáil loan.[9]

Mirroring the wider population, most of the priests who supported the revolutionary movement confined their actions to the realm of the political. A few offered more. Patrick Doyle, in addition to ghost-writing the propagandistic prison memoir of Padraic Fleming, *In Maryboro' and Mountjoy*, allowed Knockbeg College in Carlow, of which he was rector, to be used as a safe house. While Tom Burke, curate at Shrule on the border of Galway and Mayo,[10] was even more unusual in that he acted as a 'chaplain' to the local IRA brigade.[11]

Perhaps T. Keappock, a curate at Collinstown in Meath,[12] was most typical of all however, expressing his sympathies in small donations whether to the county feis or that £6 to Michael Collins.[13]

A receipt for Fr Delahunty

Fr P.H. Delahunty, curate in Callan, was the President of the South Kilkenny Comhairle Ceanntair of Sinn Féin. In addition to collecting money for Dáil Éireann, Delahunty actively supported the local IRA. In late 1920 he was arrested, court-martialled and imprisoned.

Military Archive, IE/MA/CP/06/03/01

JUNE, 1920.

Thursday 24

Roscommon N.
£830 per Dr Clynn
Drumlion

Misc Places Eng   £6.
(J. Terry)
Belfast   23   (it gets)
Tyrone South
   Dungannon   195   Per Dr McGuirk
   Coalisland   201
   Separate app   25   421

Tyrone Mid
   £23   per Seanoshan

JUNE, 1920.

Friday 25

£26. 7. 6 per Rev Canon Doyle.
         Suspense.

Clare East
   255. 10.   Suspense
         per D O Kennedy
Cavan East.
   268. 10.   D O Connell
Misc Places }
   England } £5.

Diary, 25 June 1920

Collins's diary emphasises that priests were among the most important local agents of the Dáil Loan.

National Archives, 2021/110/3

Electors of St. Patrick's Division

Who is it that claims your Vote for the assertion of Ireland's right to complete Independence ?

Read the following Extract from the Letter of an Irish Priest—

"I had the privilege of making the acquaintance of the COUNTESS DE MARKIEVICZ while she awaited in Kilmainham Prison the result of her Courtmartial. These were terrible days. Already eight executions had taken place in that prison yard, whence she could hear distinctly the volleys that robbed her of some dear friend. The strain was almost unbearable, but she found strength and solace in the consolations of religion."

"At this first meeting I gave her a little crucifix which seemed to have a very soothing effect on her; and when I gave her a Rosary Beads she expressed the greatest pleasure. —We said the Rosary regularly at the College of Surgeons! she said."

"To Councillor Partridge, who had charge of the Devotions in the College of Surgeons, she dedicated a beautiful poem on the Rosary, in which she said as they knelt around the Altar :

> "One hope, one prayer,
> Filled all our hearts, one perfect holy faith,
> Lifted our souls. As we knelt humbly there
> Your silvery voice, soft as a dying breath,
> Was answered by a hundred strong and clear;
> Craving a grace from her whom all hold dear:
> "Mary, be with us at the hour of death."

"I like to esteem the Countess a personal friend for whom I have the highest regard and deepest respect. She is really a most beautiful character, and a woman of great faith and most religious mind."

After reading such testimony by a priest regarding the fitness of Constance De Markievicz to be the representative of St. Patrick's Division when the claim for the FREEDOM OF IRELAND is being made before the Council of the Nations of the World, can you hesitate to

·: Vote for the Countess :·

Published by M. Noyk, Solicitor, Election Agent for the Candidate, College Green, Dublin; and Printed by H. & M. WOODS, High St., Dublin

Electors of St Patrick's Division

In this handbill Sinn Féin deployed quotations from an anonymous priest to vouch for Countess Markievicz with the voters of Dublin.

National Library of Ireland, EPH C2

Dáil Éireann.

Seoltap Litpeaca cun Runaiτσe Dáil Épeann, f/c Tige an Ápτο-Ιηaoip, Ác-Cliat.

Correspondence may be addressed to the Secretary, Dáil Éireann, c/o Mansion House, Dublin.

6 Sraid Fhearchair,

ATH-CLIATH.

Meadhon Foghmhair a 30, 1919.

To
Each Member of Dail Eireann.

A chara,

RE DAIL EIREANN LOAN.

I enclose you copy of the general circular which is being issued in cases where we are approaching individuals with a view to getting applications in the above. You will see that the slip which is attached to this circular is likely to increase your responsibilities.

If you will let me have a hundred, or as many more names as you wish, of likely subscribers in your Constituency, I will forward a copy of this circular with the Prospectus to each.

You might also, at the earliest possible date, but not later than Monday next, send up for the information of the Finance Committee, a statement of what has already been done in your Constituency in connection with the Loan generally, and particularly as to the number of promises handed in.

Every day our best and keenest supporters are emphasising the vital importance of making the Loan a huge success. Dr.Fogarty is laying particular emphasis on this, so too are other Divines and friends and well-wishers in England, in America, in Australia, and in other lands. The responsibility for its success rests firstly on us.

Mise,

Miceál O'Coleain

AIRE AIRGID.

F.14. 29/8/19.

Collins to 'Each Member of Dáil Éireann', 30 September 1920

In pushing his colleagues to make the Loan a success, Collins emphasised the support of members of the hierarchy, most importantly Bishop Michael Fogarty.

'WORKED ALL DAYS CLEARED ALL ARREARS'

'WORKED ALL DAY CLEARED ALL ARREARS'

These years took their toll. A police description of him as 'a young man of fair complexion clean shaven strong jaws and features' from December 1916 had changed by 1920 to a Collins 'Broad and heavy in build. Weighs 12 or 13 stone. Must have been a powerful man a few years ago; now heavy in movement and greatly out of condition. Coarse, pale face with heavy jowl...Except for the eyes he is now quite unlike earlier photograph. Looks about 40.'[1] He was 30. When he died one British newspaper rather cruelly described his 'rather rotund figure and double chin'.[2] His diaries can perhaps explain why.

Lunch is a word that appears often in the diaries, but in 1921 and 1922, as he emerged as a public politician, he seemed to be lunching for Ireland both at home and abroad. 'Tuesday lunch @ 1.30 Devonshire', 'Luncheon Shelbourne @ 1.30 Monday', 'Lunch today Hayden Talbot' hint at why he had to write to Callaghan's outfitters on 5 August 1922 to make alterations to his new uniform because 'it is too tight at the waist and neck'.[3]

But the changes in him were due more to the burden of work. His diaries are a record of constant work, of long days, short nights, the back and forth to London, the trains to Granard, the 'night mail Dublin 4am', the '2.45 mail', the '5.10 Broadstone', the 'Night mail to Ath Cliath'.[4] 'Worked all Day Cleared all arrears' suggests something of the relief of that one day when everything seemed to get done.[5] A clear day was rare enough to be worthy of remark. 'Taken off' appears twice in his diary in early 1922.[6] One was three days before the vote on the Treaty, the other was the day he became head of the Provisional Government, neither could have been restful, easy days.

And like many busy people all this work must have come at a cost to his health. He admitted to being 'In bed with cold' on 24 February 1922. The next day, though he was 'In bed also', the meetings just came to him instead.[7] They came again the day after when he was 'up for a while'.[8] Although he had to cancel a trip to Cork in June 1922, again due to a 'bad cold', 'ap mtg 6.45' still kept him at work.[9] We know from other sources that he often slept poorly, that 'stomach and kidney problems...could leave him bedridden or functioning in great discomfort', but his diaries disclose far more about his troubles with his teeth.[10] Bouts of dental appointments in September 1918, what seem to be two appointments on 9 January 1919 and again to the dentist the next day, give us a Collins at the mercy of toothache and in the hands of a hopefully benign dentist.[11] By 1922 enough photographs show the teeth he had lost.

On 14 April 1919 Collins's diary noted 'Stopped cigarets [sic] today'.[12] Maybe it was for the good of his health or having just become Secretary for Finance in the Dáil Cabinet, he thought a minister of the Irish Republic should not be seen with a cigarette in his mouth. He did not record how long his abstinence lasted. Maybe 1919 was not the best time to give up.

12th. April, 1921.

PRESIDENT

     I was reading the papers the other day about your "No smoking" decree, and since then I happened to be in some of the Government offices, and I cannot say that what you have said has had much effect on them. Seriously, I think smoking ought to be forbidden in the Government offices - at least forbidden during certain hours. It must have a damaging effect on people who go into any of our offices and see the idea taken no notice of.

M. C

Michael Collins to Eamon de Valera, 12 April 1921

Perhaps grown zealous by abstinence, Collins seemed keen that the 'No smoking' decree be adhered to, not least because non-compliance looked bad.

National Archives, DE/2/244

↑
London and North Western Railway poster

Throughout the Treaty negotiations and frequently in 1922, Collins made the exhausting crossings on the mail boat in the early hours, and then took the train on to London.

National Museum of Ireland, F:2007.109

→
Description of Michael Collins, October 1920

Though dated 4 June 1921, this description of Collins was based on observations made in October 1920. The work and the pressure had made their mark.

National Archives, London, W035/206/35

COLLINS. Michael. Woodfield, Clonakilty, Co. Cork.
8, Beechwood Avenue, Ranelagh, Dublin.
Also. Gresham Hotel, Sackville St. (Ref. D.M.P. 8-4-'22.)

Latest Description:- Height about 5'8". Broad and heavy in build.
4-6-21. Weighs 12 or 13 stone. Must have been a powerful man a few years ago; now heavy in movement
and greatly out of condition. Coarse, pale face
with heavy jowl. Clean shaven. Looks like a publican. Eyes, stern; and have a purpose in them.
Over hanging eyebrows. Except for the eyes he is
now quite unlike earlier photograph. Looks about
40. Now wears a moustache. (October 1920)

Age, 35.

ELECTED SINN FEIN M.P. FOR N. M. W. S. and S-E. CORK, MAY 1921. and
CO. ARMAGH.

Minister of Finance, Dail Eireann.

Appointed Minister of Finance under Dail's New Executive, 10th January 1922.

Member I.R.B. (One of the Chiefs).

Is the Virtual Head of the I.R.A. (Official Document stated he was
G.O.C.-in C.)

Was formerly Adjutant-General.

Elected Member of Provisional Government, IRISH FREE STATE, 14-1-22.
_Delegate at the "Three Party Conference" held at the Colonial Office,
London on 29-3-'22. (Extract from 'Irish Times', 30-3-'22.)_

A native of Woodfield, Clonakilty, Co. Cork, and a member of a very
disloyal family.

His brother JOHN, of Woodfield, Clonakilty, is interned at Bere
Island.
Has two sisters. Mrs Powell, Cork. and Sister Jerra, Convent of Mercy, Eudaleigh, Hull.
At one time employed in the Post Office, London, but apparently re-
signed as prior to the "Great War" he was a bank clerk to the
"Guarantee Trust Company, New York" and 32, Lombard Street, London.

Came to Dublin early in 1916 and was employed as temporary clerk by
CRAIG GARDNER & Co, apparently to evade Military Service.

Became a member of the Irish Volunteers in Dublin.

Took part in the Rebellion of 1916, was arrested and deported to
England.

Released at the General Amnesty, August 1916.

After his release he lived at 44, Mountjoy Street, Dublin, and became Paid Secretary to the Sinn Fein Organisation.

Was interned at Frongoch in 1916 and released 23-12-16 when he took
a most active and prominent part in organising the I.R.A.

Took part in the Longford Election Campaign, April 1917.

/In June 1917

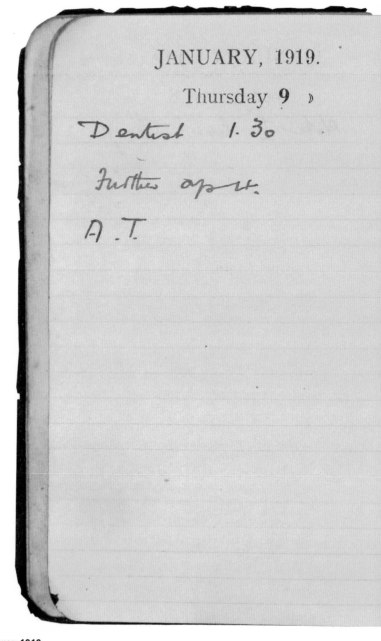

JANUARY, 1919.
Thursday 9 ☽

Dentist   1. 30

Further appt.

A . T

Diary, 9–10 January 1919

His humour cannot have been helped by his periodic bouts of toothache.

National Archives, 2021/110/2

Friday 10

1. 30 Dentist

12. m. with H

wrote Sean to
keep ap.

↑
Menu for dinner at the Gresham Hotel, Dublin, celebrating the release of Seán MacEoin, 17 August 1921

The truce brought its moments of ease, and this signed menu captures the camaraderie, something of the enjoyment, as well as the turbot and the soufflé maraschino.

National Library of Ireland, Ms 33,642/1

→
Bronislava Nijinska as the Humming Bird Princess in 'The sleeping princess', London, November 1921

THE 'BIG FELLA' AT THE BALLET

THE 'BIG FELLA' AT THE BALLET

Collins began 1918 at a new year's night concert in the Mansion House.[1] The last word he wrote in his 1922 diary was 'Mass'.[2] His five diaries give us only glimpses of this sociable man's social life, but even in the crumbs he leaves us we can see change.

Some of that change was natural, perhaps appropriate. A single man in his twenties might dance one Saturday night away after another at a 'U.C.D. Camóg Céilide', at a 'University Gaelic Society' dance; a man in his thirties, with position and a fiancée, has less time and necessity for such lively weekends.[3] In this he was little different from his colleagues and friends. Though he noted only one wedding in his diary—'Paul D. Cusack married today'—the many wedding photographs of the Irish revolution suggest Sinn Féin concerts and Gaelic League céilithe bristled with passion and romance.[4] Alternatively, for Collins and many like him, their revolutions coincided with that age and instinct to settle down to a quieter social life.

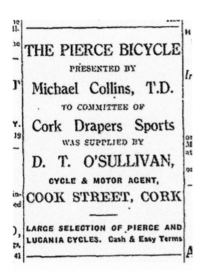

THE PIERCE BICYCLE

PRESENTED BY

Michael Collins, T.D.

TO COMMITTEE OF

Cork Drapers Sports

WAS SUPPLIED BY

D. T. O'SULLIVAN,

CYCLE & MOTOR AGENT,

COOK STREET, CORK

LARGE SELECTION OF PIERCE AND LUCANIA CYCLES. Cash & Easy Terms

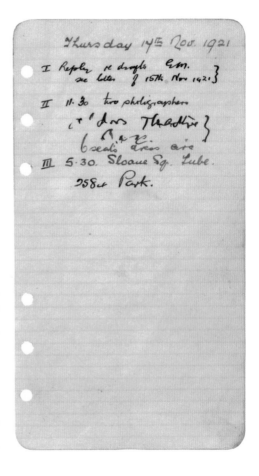

↑
Advertisement for D.T. O'Sullivan, cycle and motor agent, Cork, *Cork Examiner*, 28 June 1922

His interests were certainly varied. On 23 June 1922 Collins made a note in his diary of 'Drapers Sports Prize'. He provided a bicycle as a prize for the five-mile cycling open handicap at the 'Cork Drapers' Sports' held at the Mardyke Cricket Grounds. O'Sullivan lost no time in advertising himself as supplier to Collins.

Courtesy of the Irish Examiner

←
'Ballinalee Hero Weds'

A still from a newsreel reporting on the wedding of Seán MacEoin and Alice Cooney on 21 June 1922 captures Collins joking with the bride and groom.

Courtesy of British Pathé, Film Id: 272.08

↑
Diary, 17 November 1921

With some of the British negotiators in Liverpool at the National Unionist Association Conference on 17 November, there was time for an evening at the ballet.

National Archives, 2021/110/4

A Stáck   6th June 1919

A cáraí

I am very grievously to blame for not having written for almost a fortnight. Things have been in a greater rush than ever and as a matter of fact there were two other incidents like the Moloney one. They took a good deal of time and are not yet complete. Also I'm fed up. Things are not going very smoothly – although perhaps that's too strong an expression. All sorts of miserable little under-currents are working and the effect is anything but good. However when I'm feeling in better mood I'll write you more of these things.

You will see some stuff in today's 'Freeman' about proposals also made by the American delegates — these should not be taken seriously. We have no knowledge of them. As likely as not the very subject matter has suffered in this instance at the hands of the censor.

The main activity this week has been in the matrimonial line — Monday – Dick Mulcahy & Miss M Ryan

Michael Collins to Austin Stack, 6 June 1919

Like many in their late twenties, Collins was struck by the number of his friends and contemporaries getting married.

National Library of Ireland, Ms 5,848/19

By 1922, as head of the Provisional Government, he had to be more mindful of where he went and with whom he was seen. Newspapers noted his attendance at the performance of the Vatican Choirs at La Scala in Dublin on a Monday in May.[5] He had become a person whose attendance was assiduously noted; he had become 'a social sight'.[6]

Whether he enjoyed sacred music or went because 'his betrothed', as the *Irish Independent* called Kitty Kiernan, was keen to go, there is no way to know.[7]

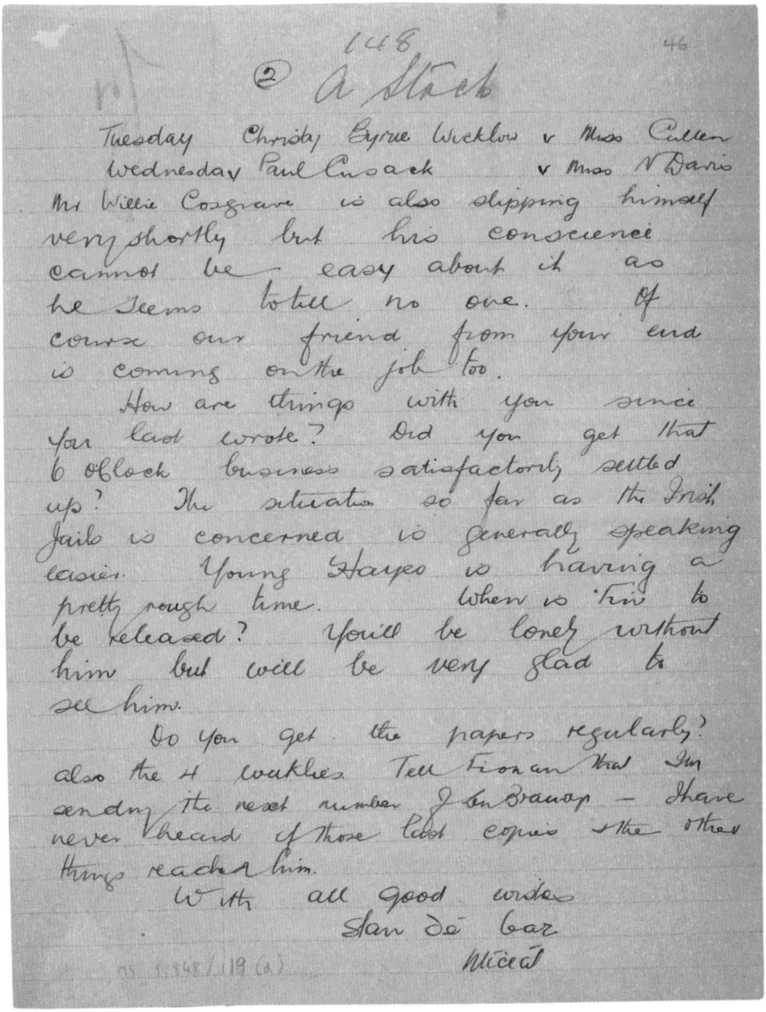

148 46

② A Stack

Tuesday Christy Byrne Wicklow v Miss Cullen
Wednesday Paul Cusack v Miss N Davis
Mr Willie Cosgrave is also slipping himself
very shortly but his conscience
cannot be easy about it as
he seems to tell no one. Of
course our friend from your end
is coming on the job too.
How are things with you since
you last wrote? Did you get that
6 o'clock business satisfactorily settled
up? The situation so far as the Irish
Jails is concerned is generally speaking
easier. Young Hayes is having a
pretty rough time. When is 'Fin' to
be released? You'll be lonely without
him but will be very glad to
see him.
Do you get the papers regularly?
also the 4 weeklies. Tell Fionan that I'm
sending the next number of An Branar – I have
never heard if those last copies & the other
things reached him.
With all good wishes
Slan do bar
Mícéal

But his diaries, read together with other sources, suggest a taste for culture that took him far beyond céilithe at the Mansion House or the side-lines at Croke Park. There were greater depths to the man said to have ended a party at Hans Place on 10 November 1921 by throwing food and coal with his IRA and IRB pals.[8] 'The beggar's opera' may have enthralled or bored him in London in October 1921; he may have fidgeted impatiently in his seat at 'The sleeping princess' performed by Serge Diaghilev's Les Ballets Russes in November 1921, but he was there, the

'Big Fella' at the ballet, there at some of London's most distinguished and popular productions whether he liked them or not.[9] In the years of his London youth, he had been a regular theatre-goer, so even in his '"blast and bloody" stage of adolescent evolution' he prized the plays of G.B. Shaw and J.M. Barrie, he read his Conrad and his Hardy just as well.[10]

Whatever he made of the ballet and the opera in 1921, those evenings were sociable affairs. Six tickets were bought for the dress circle at London's Alhambra Theatre for 'The sleeping princess', and he signed the programme for 'The beggar's opera' along with Arthur Griffith, Éamonn and May Duggan, with Hannie Collins, Kitty Kiernan, and Mable Hopkins.[11] Sometimes the company means as much as the singing and the music.

Because it is Collins there is a temptation to read more than we ought into the things he sought chiefly to enjoy. When he took his seat at 'The whiteheaded boy' in the Abbey in January 1918 he may have done so because the leading man was Arthur Shields, veteran of the GPO and fellow Frongoch internee, but on a dark Saturday evening in January Collins might just have wanted to sit surrounded by others, to see a humorous, well-received play.[12]

The 'bookish' teenager his sister Hannie remembered, grew into the man who recorded visits to the 'Library' in his diaries, who prompted himself to 'Call at Hodges Figges' [sic] bookshop in 1918.[13] After taking over Dublin Castle in January 1922, he wanted to see or create a catalogue of the Castle's books by March.[14] Even if his reading 'regularly out-distanced his powers of reflection' as Frank O'Connor rather cattily remarked, like many busy people he may have read as much for pleasure as to be thought smart.[15]

His diaries record no galleries, no gramophone records, no evenings at the pictures in the dark. They only take us to appointments, to meetings, to the threshold of La Scala, but they don't let us pry inside. There's no talk, no drink, no friendship; we hear nothing of what happened when the work was over, when the meetings were done. Those nights, and the worlds that must have been put to rights on the way home, remain his own.

Michael Collins posing for the camera, London, October 1921

LONDON

LONDON

On 3 December 1921 Michael Collins wrote to Kitty Kiernan on headed paper from 10 Downing Street. 'Dear Kitty, Will you please look at the address – I am actually writing here'.[1] After almost two months of negotiations and three days before signing a treaty in London, he was still impressed by that address. It was a long way from Woodfield to Downing Street.

His 1921 and 1922 diaries have their share of daunting London addresses: '2 Whitehall G[ar]d[en]s' the offices of the Cabinet; the 'Treasury Board Room'; the 'Colonial Office'; Lord Birkenhead's room in the 'H[ouse] of Lords'; 'Chancell[or's] Room'; the rather cryptic '509 room'; 'Churchills [sic] room'; '2 Sussex G[ar]d[en]s', Churchill's home; '32 Gros[venor] G[ar]d[e]n[s]', Birkenhead's house; and always back to Downing Street.[2] And these new addresses brought new, formidable names: 'Lloyd Geo. Chamb & Lord B.', 'Beatty & Churchill', 'Evans & Chetwood [sic]', again 'Lloyd G & Birk'.[3] With no elaboration such diary entries sum up how much his position had altered from his last diary entries of 1920. The 'blood-thirsty chief of a murder gang' as many British newspapers had styled him through late 1920 and into 1921, had arrived, as Collins said himself, 'into the spotlight of a London conference' in October 1921. Then 'the legendary figure' of the war of independence was transformed, whether he wanted to be or not, into a public figure, into an international statesman.[4] The diaries give us little more than these names and these addresses, but they reflect just how much Collins's life and work had irrevocably changed.

With that spotlight came a natural curiosity. In a letter to Kitty in the early days of the negotiations in October 1921 he seemed bemused by it: 'You'll have seen the praise and flattery that has been showered on me since I came here and have been publicly known. You will know I hope that they leave me untouched just as their dispraise and their blame did. All the same to me. That upper lip of mine has been called on to do much scornful upturning since I've seen you.'[5] By 16 November he wrote to her that 'the *Tatler* has asked me to give them a sitting for a photograph' and his diary of 17 November would suggest that he had agreed to play along: '11.30 two photographers' came and got their photographs.[6] He wrote in his diary 'Augustus John 28 Mallord St Chelsea' on 26 November.[7] Sir John Lavery had already begun his portrait—'I sat today for my portrait – my interesting life!'—but, in noting Augustus John's name and Chelsea

Leaving 10 Downing Street after the first day of negotiations, 11 October 1921

Crowds cheered the Irish delegation when they entered Downing Street. Although Griffith seemed buoyant, 'on the whole we have scored today', Collins seems less sure of his step.

National Library of Ireland, NPA MKN33

address, Collins was clearly tempted by the thought of sitting for the artist who had painted Lawrence of Arabia in 1919.[8]

His diaries record a new friendship presumably borne out of the same curiosity. Sir James Barrie, the novelist and playwright, first appeared in Collins's diary on 14 October 1921 and they continued to meet through those tense last months of 1921 and again in London in 1922.[9] Lavery described their friendship as 'odd moments', but the diaries' 'Ring up J.M. Barry [sic]', 'Lunch with Sir JB', 'Sir Jas Barrie – to ring him up', '? Ap[pointment] Sir Jas Barrie', '12.45 to 1 Sir JB' imply the time spent with Barrie was time Collins enjoyed.[10] Barrie's plays had been among his favourites as a young theatre-goer in London, so even the hardened revolutionary must have been thrilled to spend time with the man who invented Peter Pan.[11]

This becoming a public figure in London was certainly used against Collins by those who later took an anti-Treaty stance. As early as November 1921 rumours of 'rowdy and drunken conduct at Hans Place' and 'the name of Michael Collins bandied about as central figure in alleged orgies' could be heard, but his diaries give little cause to substantiate such accusations and claims.[12] Instead they order out his London days and nights predominantly in conferences, meetings and work. The Treaty negotiations, which began on 11 October and ended on 6 December 1921, were not, as we might assume, uniform days of negotiation and discussion.[13] Meetings were conducted around the day-to-day business of British government. The 1921 diary, which only began on the second day of the talks, notes Downing Street meetings at various different times, at 11.00, 3.30, 5.00.[14] 'Meeting Downing St @ 5 Followed by Special sub-Conference on General Question', 'Truce m[ee] t[in]g at 3.00', '5.30 Delegation', 'Ap @ 11.30 Treasury' are just a small sample of the plethora of side meetings that were a part of the negotiations.[15] The schedule of 13 October 1921 sums up the pressures and movement of these days. It began with 'Gen[era]l Confer[ence]' at 11.00, which 'adj[ourne]d @1.15'. Then it was on to a meeting with Lord Beatty and Winston Churchill at the Colonial Office. Then '4.30 Truce C[ommi]ttee Over 7 O'C' and then back to prepare for the next day's work.[16]

The diaries confirm what we have long known: the singling out of Arthur Griffith and Collins from the rest of the plenipotentiaries by the Prime Minister David Lloyd George. Collins's note in his diary of 'Memo presented to us A[rthur] G[riffith] & I see Lloyd G & Birk Latters [sic] room H of Lords' of 27 October 1921 simply corroborates that.[17] What Collins thought of it all he kept for his letters home. In those he admitted 'I am lonely and very very discontented'; in those he confessed 'I wish to God I were back home'.[18] In his diary he just kept going: '11 O'C L.Geo Etc!'[19] He said a lot with an etc and an exclamation mark.

Arthur Griffith wrote of the unevenness of these London days. 'I was working from 11am to half past one in the morning. Other days are quite slack.'[20] The 'slack' days Collins filled with old familiar names, with 'S.A.M.' or Sam Maguire, with Art O'Brien, with 'Frank F.' or 'Frank Fitz', perhaps Desmond Fitzgerald's brother, an old hand at buying and smuggling arms for the IRA.[21] He also noted IRA addresses, and they remind us, if reminder is needed, that this increasingly public statesman still had his revolutionary side. As early as 17 October 1921 his

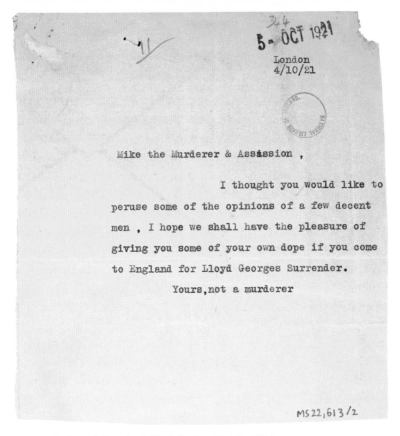

London
4/10/21

Mike the Murderer & Assássion ,

I thought you would like to
peruse some of the opinions of a few decent
men , I hope we shall have the pleasure of
giving you some of your own dope if you come
to England for Lloyd Georges Surrender.

Yours,not a murderer

MS 22,613 /2

A threatening letter delivered to Collins in London, 4 October 1921

The authors of this and other threatening letters showed the strength of feeling toward Collins, fostered in part by the British press. The political risk for Lloyd George in undertaking the negotiations is also clear.

National Library of Ireland, Ms 22,613/2

diary recorded an appointment at '8 Sterndale Road @ 8.30'.[22] The home of the Cullinane family in West Kensington, 8 Sterndale Road was where Manchester IRA man, William O'Keeffe, remembered meeting Reginald Dunne, officer commanding the London IRA in 1921.[23] Dunne, along with Joseph O'Sullivan, would kill Sir Henry Wilson outside his home in Belgravia's Eaton Place on 22 June 1922.[24] The British government's response to Wilson's murder left Collins with little choice but civil war. Why Collins visited Sterndale Road, we can only surmise. The temptation might be to draw a line from Collins's visit to the events of 22 June, but his diary is silent on whom he met or what happened there.

As head of the Provisional Government Collins returned several times to London in 1922. His diary entry of 6 February 1922 provides the detail of one of these later London days. It began in Downing Street at 10am, then to see Hannie, then to Argyll Road.[25] Next he went to Lord Birkenhead's home at Grosvenor Gardens, then to meet Crompton Llewelyn Davies, before the Colonial Office at 4.15. At 5.30, with Eamon Duggan, he saw Roger Casement's diary in the House of Lords. An hour later he was back in Downing Street, then to his hotel, the Jermyn Court, for a conference 're Procedure' to end the day.[26] The pace was just as fierce as late 1921, and, arguably the tenor of the meetings was just as furious. His electoral pact with de Valera prompted disgust in London. To Churchill it was 'an outrage upon democratic principles', while the draft of the Free State constitution was to Lloyd George a 'complete evasion and negation of the Treaty'.[27] For both Collins was brought to heel at London meetings, prompting dispirited letters home.[28] 'These two days have been the worse [sic] I have ever spent', 'It would be so pleasant to be relieved of all responsibility', 'Things are serious – far far more serious than anyone at home thinks', 'I wish to God someone else was in the position and not I'.[29] Again, his diaries show nothing of this dejection. They record the work but not the peace of mind it cost.

Michael Collins to Eamon de Valera, 11 July 1921

The nephews of Crompton Llewelyn Davies had inspired Barrie's 'Peter Pan'. The Llewelyn Davies connection may have prompted Barrie's interest in Ireland and then in Collins. Many other prominent figures in London, including T.E. Lawrence and George Bernard Shaw, shared this interest.

National Archives, DE/2/244

11 July 1921.

President.

     My feeling about the visit is that you should time
it for Friday next - that seems to me to be the longest we
can delay, and a preliminary Meeting for Friday would
naturally reassemble on the following Tuesday.

     Sir James Barrie, Adelphi Terrace House, will be
pleased to put up the Irish Leaders at his Flat there.
Attached is his note to my friend. He is the author of
"Peter Pan", and he says he is known to fame as "the man
lives opposite Bernard Shaw - Of course, you know Bernard
Shaw does live opposite Sir James Barrie.

     Barrie is, I am told, a good fellow and his
invitation is certainly quite genuine. We should at least
thank him for the offer. If you wish me to write to him
I shall do so.

DÁIL ÉIREANN.

TIGH LAIGHEAN
(Leinster House),

BAILE ÁTHA CLIATH
(Dublin).

Michael Collins & I saw the Casement diary by arrangement with Lord Birkenhead. We read it. I did not know Casement's handwriting. Collins did. He said it was his. The diary was in two parts – bound volumes – repeating ad nauseam details of sex perversion – of the personal appearance and beauty of native boys – with special reference to

---

Statement by Éamonn Duggan on reading the Casement diary with Michael Collins, undated [c. early 1930s]

The certainty with which Collins authenticated the diary, Deirdre McMahon argues, left 'the new Free State government diffident about approaching the British for the return of Casement's body'.

National Library of Ireland, Ms 17,601/6/1

a certain portion of their anatomy.

It was disgusting.

There was nothing to suggest that it was a copy of another man's diary.

Collins was satisfied that it was Casement's. So was Birkenhead.

At a later date someone who had surreptitious recourse to the diary wrote a book – a life of Casement

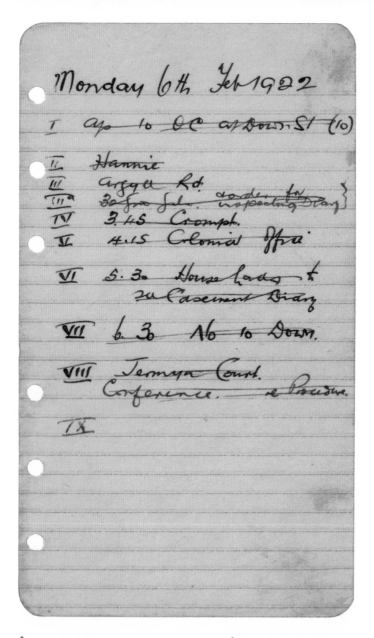

Diary, 6 February 1922

A long day in London included Downing Street, the Colonial Office, a trip to 'see Casement Diary', and meeting Hannie.

National Archives, 2021/110/5

Nevil Macready and General Strickland

This cartoon by Shemus (Ernest Forbes) represents General Nevil Macready and General Peter Strickland, general officer commanding Sixth Division. Strickland complained of the truce, 'This d_____d effort at peace [is] much more arduous than the other thing.'

National Library of Ireland, PD 4309 TX 228

THE TRUCE

'3O'C @ 2 Whitehall Gds'.[1] On 12 October 1921 this, the first entry on the first day of Collins's renewed diary, recorded the first meeting of the Committee on the Observance of the Truce. He led the Irish representatives while the British team was accompanied by Sir Nevil Macready, general officer commanding in Ireland.[2] Macready, who had not met Collins before, was quick to tell colleagues that he was 'a great disappointment'.[3]

Barbs and disappointments aside, the committee's purpose was to ensure that the plenary conference did not become bogged down in lengthy discussions about the keeping, and the breaching, of the truce. It was largely successful, though the plenary session of 17 October—'Conference 3.30 No.10. Down St.'[4] —heard lengthy protests from the Irish delegation, including a complaint from Collins that he had been 'shadowed at Mass at Maiden Lane yesterday'.[5]

The committee met five times, twice in the early days and on three occasions in early November.[6] By then the question of Ulster had ensnared the negotiations.[7] Consequently, on Saturday 12 November Collins reported to de Valera, 'Practically speaking no progress has been made since last week-end. . . We are concerned principally with a couple of important Truce breakage cases'.[8]

His diaries reflect this latter preoccupation. On Tuesday 1 November, the day of the third meeting, Collins wrote 'Wicklow Policeman Shooting Case', 'Note re Spike Island Interment Camp', 'Billeting Cases' and 'Col. Peacock's place'.[9] Each was an item on the committee's agenda.[10] Collins consistently used the body to raise the treatment of prisoners and internees, while the British were roiled by the recent wounding of a Constable McCarthy, out for a Sunday stroll on Weaver Square, Baltinglass, County Wicklow, with two colleagues and some girls,[11] as well as the occupation of the farm of W.J. Peacock at Innishannon, Cork. The IRA had killed Peacock on 1 June.[12]

On 5 November, when Collins noted 'Memo re Rathkeale' he referred to the billeting case that would prove most contentious.[13] During early exchanges at the committee meeting of the previous day, 4 November, Collins had insisted that it would be breach of the truce if, as threatened, the British army occupied Rathkeale workhouse.[14] In contrast, Sir Laming Worthington Evans, secretary of state for war, 'desired it to be placed on record that he could not waive his right to occupy public buildings for use as winter quarters'.[15] Back in Dublin, de Valera and Cathal Brugha decided too that it was a matter of principle: 'the workhouses are

Rathkeale, rural west Limerick

National Library of Ireland, L_CAB_09082

the property of the people'.[16] Perhaps as importantly, this particular one was in the possession of the local IRA and they insisted it would be of strategic importance if hostilities resumed.[17] When, on 25 November, the British army appeared intent upon carrying out their plan to take over the building, the IRA evacuated and burned it down at 2am.[18] Their actions had the practical consequence of rendering the building uninhabitable while, 'property of the people' or not, they had given the hated workhouse over to the 'symbolically purifying effect' of fire.[19]

Collins may have been in Whitehall but Rathkeale was on his mind, at least some of the time. And his diaries show that there were other places on other days—'Tipperary' and 'Rath', 'Kesh' and 'Belfast'[20]—testifying to the gap between the word 'truce' and the state of Ireland, north and south, in the final months of 1921.

S.F.C.3.

SECRET

S.F.C.3.

CONFERENCE ON IRELAND

COMMITTEE ON THE OBSERVANCE OF THE TRUCE
held at 2 Whitehall Gardens S.W., on
Wednesday, October 12th, 1921, at 3 p.m.

PRESENT

BRITISH REPRESENTATIVES   IRISH REPRESENTATIVES

Sir L.Worthington Evans   Mr.M.Collins,

Sir Hamar Greenwood   Mr.R.C.Barton,

                                  Mr.E.J.Duggan,

                                  Mr.Art O'Brien

THERE WERE ALSO PRESENT

Sir J.Anderson

Mr.A.Cope

General Sir N.Macready

General Tudor.

Mr.T.Jones)
)............................British Secretaries.
Mr.L.Curtis)

                        Mr.E.Childers,

                           Irish Secretary.

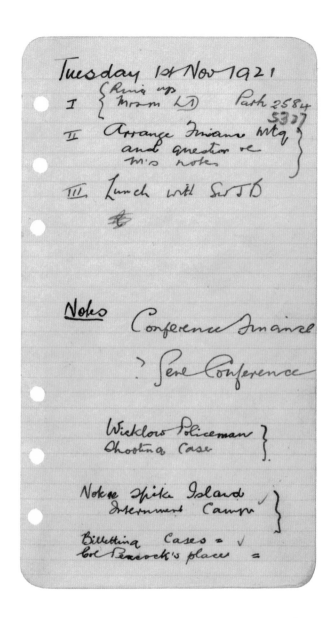

Tuesday 1st Nov 1921

I { Ring up
     mom LD   Parth 2584
                           533?

II Arrange Finance Mtg
    and question re
    m's notes

III Lunch with Sir JB

Notes

Conference Finance

? Sere Conference

Wicklow Policeman }
Shooting Case   }

Notes Spike Island ✓
Internment Camp   }

Billeting Cases = ✓
Col Peacock's place   =

←

**Minute of Committee on the Observance
of the Truce, 12 October 1921**

In addition to the cabinet ministers and usual secretaries, the British team at
the first meeting of the Committee on the Observance of the Truce included
Sir John Anderson and Alfred Cope, key figures at Dublin Castle, General Hugh
Tudor, who had effective control of policing in Ireland, and Nevil Macready.

National Archives, DE/2/304/1/10

↑

**Diary, 1 November
1921**

National Archives,
2021/110/4

OGLAIG NA h-EIREANN

ORD OIFIG, AT CLIAT.   GENERAL HEADQUARTERS

DUBLIN.

10th Nov., 1921.

Department...C/S

Reference No. M.422

TO: MICK.

1.   RATHKEALE WORKHOUSE: The President spoke to myself and
the Minister for Defence this evening with regard to
Workhouses and he takes up the attitude that we must main-
tain that the Workhouses are the property of the people, and
that "the guardians of the poor in the district are the real
owners."   They have come to some legal decision on this
point and he asked the Minister for Defence to have you sent
a copy of this decision.
According to his ruling we cannot evacuate the Rathkeale
Workhouse, in order to allow the Enemy in.
Further, as a counter-offensive in this matter he has
arranged that the Minister for Defence will get the Minister
for Local Government to get the guardians of any Workhouse
into which the Enemy have gone since the Truce, to send him
(the Minister for Local Government) particulars of the case,
with a view to having our Chief Liaison Officer demand
evacuation.........

(SIGNED)._____CHIEF OF STAFF.

↑
**Richard Mulcahy to Michael
Collins, 10 November 1921**

Mulcahy updated Collins, in London, on the thinking
in Dublin regarding Rathkeale workhouse.

Military Archives, IE-MA-LE-29

→
**A cracked photograph of
Michael Collins in uniform**

National Library of Ireland, KE 13

COMING
TOGETHER,
COMING
APART

COMING TOGETHER, COMING APART

On 27 February 1919 Collins wrote an unusually long entry. Many diarists write not simply to record events or conversations but as a way of thinking these through. Collins sometimes treated letters in this way, but rarely his diaries.

On this occasion, however, he tried to put an order on what 'Mr Kelly' said about 'Organ[isation] Britain'.[1] Following the formation of Dáil Éireann, a support organisation in Britain was on the agenda in early 1919. Patrick J. Kelly had ideas he wanted to advance and, as always, Collins wanted to know, and influence, what was going on.

A vigorous participant at the radical end of Irish nationalist politics in Liverpool, and a city councillor from 1914, Kelly had come to support Sinn Féin. Collins noted three aspects of his position at that February meeting: the new body should be 'composed of all existing organisations', should 'take part in internal politics in England', and that there was a 'tendency toward sectarianism in his explanation'. This sounds just like Kelly, formed in the sectarian politics of Liverpool while being committed to both trade unionism and social reform.[2] A month later, at a meeting in Manchester, Kelly was elected first chairman of the Irish Self-Determination League of Great Britain (ISDL).[3] But he didn't control it: Art O'Brien did.

Though Art O'Brien was eighteen years his senior, Collins came to know the older man during his early days in London. They were not close then, though they were in the Gaelic League and the Geraldines GAA club together.[4] After the Rising, O'Brien established a prisoner support group, the Irish National Relief Fund (INRF), which became the English affiliate to the INA&VDF. Consequently, he worked with Collins; first, while Collins was in Frongoch prison camp (1916) and, later, when the younger man managed the INA&VDF. Trust and respect grew.

Art O'Brien to Michael Collins, 24 October 1917

This letter illustrates the close working relationship that developed between Collins and O'Brien during 1917 as they worked together for prisoners and internees in England.

National Library of Ireland, Ms 24,324/2/18

cisce consanca éireannac.

IRISH NATIONAL RELIEF FUND.

London Branch of the Irish National Aid and Volunteer Dependants' Fund.

Cheques to be drawn to the order of the Irish National Relief Fund, and crossed "London and Provincial Bank, Holborn Branch."

Chairman :
R. MURRAY.

Vice-Chairman :
JOHN J. McGRATH.

Hon. Treasurers :
C. B. DUTTON.
JOSEPH CASSIDY.

Hon. Secretaries :
ART O'BRIEN.
J. J. FINTAN MURPHY.

Appeal Committee :
Mrs. Clement Shorter
Miss Eva Goore-Booth
Mrs. Ginnell
Mrs. Dryhurst
Mrs. Crilly
Mrs. Cavanagh
Miss Nora Walsh
Miss Agnes MacHale
Very Revd. Mgr. Canon W. F. Brown, V.G.
Revd. Dr. J. Byrne O'Connell
  „ Fr. T. O'Sullivan
  „ Fr. W. Kent, O.S.C.
  „ Fr. W. W. Leonard
  „ Fr. R. Moore
  „ Fr. B. Murphy
  „ Fr. Campbell
  „ Fr. J. M. Kearney
  „ Fr. F. Cassels
  „ Fr. O'Connor
  „ Fr. P. H. Murray
  „ Fr. W. L. O'Farrell
  „ Fr. Devine
  „ Fr. J. Thornton
  „ Fr. J. Kelly
  „ Fr. V. W. Magrath
Bro. O'Donnell
Dr. Alex. MacDonnell
  „ J. Reidy
  „ Mark Ryan
  „ O'Connell
  „ Cotter
  „ England, LL.D.
  „ M. Crowley
  „ Ml. Ryan
M. J. Fitzgerald
H. E. M. Bradley
Wm. MacCarthy
W. P. Ryan
Thos. Martin
Edward Morrissey
Robert Lynd
Owen Ward
Luke Brady
Jerh. O'Brien
J. C. Nolan
J. H. McDonnell
M. J. Doherty
Richard Murray
John J. McGrath
C. B. Dutton
J. Cassidy
J. J. Fintan Murphy
Art O'Brien

87, Fulwood House,

Fulwood Place,

Holborn,

London, W.C. 24th October, 1917.

A chara,

You will be glad to hear that we have a most satisfactory report with regard to Eamonn O'Tierney. His condition has very greatly improved within the last few weeks both physically and mentally, and we quite anticipate that the Medical Superintendent will be sufficiently satisfied with him in a few weeks time to approve of his release.

I would like all the Executive in Dublin to know that we have received the greatest possible help from Dr. Chambers in this matter. As his name has not occurred in former correspondence, I may explain that he is an Irishman from the North of Ireland, and that we were given an introduction to him from another Irish doctor.

I should also mention that Dr. Chambers is one of the best known mental specialists here, and has a very extensive practice. From the very first Dr. Chambers has shown the utmost kindness and sympathy for Eamonn, and although he has twice visited Epsom specially to see him, and has also been in correspondence with the Medical Superintendent at the Asylum, refuses to make any charge for his services, saying that although he and Eamonn O'Tierney are not of the same way of thinking politically, yet he (Eamonn O'Tierney) being a fellow Irishman and in distress over here, he was only too glad to do whatever he could for him. I hope we shall all keep Dr. Chamber's name in mind.

Is mise do chara,

Hon. Secretary.

M. Ua.Coileain.

Wednesday 26

6.30 Exc. 4 No. 11.

Re Con Crowly at Flemings.

Wed 1.30

Joe McDonagh & Dawson. ✓

Dick Connolly

Re. Org in Britain Thursday 27. 2.

Mr Kelly =

(I) Wants to take part in intern
politics in England.

(II) Suggested that the propos
organisation be composed
all existing organisation

(III) Tending towards sectaria
in his explanation ..

Diary, 27 February 1919

National Archives, 2021/110/3

Thursday 27

Vote Con for Cork. 2nd.
JJ. Thurles 4th.
Harry for Cavan }
Joe O.R & " } 2nd.
Mrs Sean Con... }

Míceál for Sligo 2nd
Beazley for **Bray** 28th Feb

3 o'clock
Seumas Hughes re R P D Papers ordered Sean T.
Caulfield

British Fleets must
hold the supremacy of the seas
to protect the Empire.. (The
Inhabitants of the British Empire
number fully ⅕ the Worlds Population)

135

In January 1919 Collins ensured that O'Brien was appointed the official representative of Sinn Féin and, then, Dáil Éireann in London, reporting to him. That post, and O'Brien's record, ensured his dominance of the ISDL.[5] In an apparent defeat for Kelly, a clause in its founding constitution stated, 'no Branch or District Committee shall at any time take any action in regard to or any part in English politics.'[6]

Collins influenced nationalist activity in Britain through other channels too, particularly the Irish Volunteers/IRA and the IRB. His diaries reflect this with references to, for instance, Joe Vize (Glasgow)[7] and Liam McMahon (Manchester),[8] but O'Brien was his most important and constant contact. The numerous diary references to O'Brien capture only a fraction of the correspondence between them. During the negotiations in London in late 1921 both made use of similar diaries and, occasionally, they both noted the same appointment or lunch. On 15 November Collins noted, 'AOB Lunch 1.30': for O'Brien it was '1.30 Lunch MOC'.[9]

Art O'Brien with the staff of the London Office of Dáil Éireann

In the back row, left to right, Seán Molloy, Maeve O'Brien and Paddy Codyre. In the front row, left to right, Liam Moore, Fintan Murphy, Art O'Brien and C.B. Dutton.

National Library of Ireland, NPA POLF 215

ciste conzanta éireannać

Irish National Relief Fund

94 Fulwood House, Fulwood Place, Holborn, W.C.

M.............................., the holder of this Card, is authorised to collect on behalf of the above Fund.

Issued by ....
Hon. Secretary.

Date .... No. ....

Objects of the Fund: To render assistance to any Irish person who may be deported to or imprisoned or interned in Great Britain, and to assist those Irish people resident in Great Britain, or formerly resident therein, and their relatives or dependants who have suffered financially owing to any operation in connection with the war.

Committee of Management:
Chairman—Richard Murray.
Vice-Chairman—John J. McGrath.
Hon. Secs.—J. J. Fintan Murphy, Art O'Brien.
Hon. Treasurers—C. B. Dutton, Joseph Cassidy.

Patrick Mahon, Yarnhall Street, Dublin.

Irish National Relief Fund collection card

Art O'Brien is listed as an honorary secretary, but it was very much he who led the organisation.

National Library of Ireland, Ms 1563/6

Their last meal was probably that recorded by O'Brien on 14 June 1922: '1.30 Lunch MOC Shelbourne'.[10] It doesn't appear in Collins's diary. By then many close relationships had come apart. The organisations they had built, they reduced to confusion. We usually describe it as a split, 'the split' even, evoking a hatchet and dry timber, but it was slower, more painful, than that. O'Brien's resentments had started to accumulate during the Treaty negotiations when his role did not meet his exaggerated expectations. When he tried to use the ISDL to promote an anti-Treaty position, he provoked pro-Treaty members, including P.J. Kelly, and soon-to-be former friends in Dublin. Inevitably, if gradually, the Provisional Government pushed him out of his post and his office. First they sent in the auditors, then they sacked him.[11]

On 2 March, when defending the probing questioning of the accountant general to O'Brien, Collins wrote, in the past tense, of 'the period in which we were working harmoniously'. Four days later O'Brien replied, 'So far as I am personally concerned, our working harmoniously did not come to an end at any time: and it does not seem to me to be any reason, because our views on certain matters are somewhat divergent that we cannot continue to work harmoniously.'[12] He can hardly have believed it, and he was certainly wrong. By 8 May he had become, for Collins, the kind of diary entry that read: 'VIII Report re Art O'Brien = London Office.'[13]

Michael Collins campaigning on a public platform, *c*. June 1922

The only one facing the photographer, Collins seems an isolated and lonely figure among the crowd.

National Library of Ireland, NPA POLF28

'WITHOUT HOPE OF UNITY'

'WITHOUT HOPE OF UNITY'

In 1950 Lar Brady remembered him writing down notes, that 'fellows jumped up and they had their say', and Collins was all the time 'taking down on a piece of paper who were for and who were against the Treaty'.[1] When Brady watched him at IRB meetings in March and April 1922, Collins was writing more in his diary than just a tally of IRB men taking sides. Brady didn't know it, but Collins described his views as 'thoughtful'; Brady's 'Question of spirit', 'Question of development' contrasted sharply with Collins's note of 'Longford – Bitter feeling' and Meath's 'Understanding not kept'.[2]

At the same meeting Collins made a note of the gloomy, the ominous and the matter-of-fact: 'O'Duffy – Without hope of unity', 'Kerry = Politics = Shooting', 'Tipperary = Stick to Republic', and his economy of words, after all the weeks of fractious talk since he signed the Treaty, is maybe telling of what mattered to him, what stuck.[3] He wrote the phrase 'Fighting each other' and then underlined it twice. Right underneath he noted 'Míceál – Do away with him' in the same neat, unflinching hand.[4] In the last throws of the Dáil debates just before the vote on the Treaty was taken, he had said 'Anything that can be said about me, say it'.[5] All the same, this 'Míceál – Do away with him' must have been quite a thing for him to hear about himself.

Such a phrase, and his note of 2 July 1922 of something someone else said, 'A[rthur] G[riffith] & M[ichael] C[ollins] will have to go round in a bird cage for the rest of their lives', might imply his 1922 diary is redolent of the rancour civil war caused, but these are rare intrusions upon the diaries' familiar restrained tone.[6] The entries were functional throughout the acrimonious Treaty debates—'Session 11. Public', 'Private Session @ 11'. They were taken up with the practical business of winning the vote: 'To ask Duffy to speak re pensions &c in Article', while 'Bavaria Etc' was a reminder that there was something in Professor Stockley's speech against the Treaty worth thinking about.[7] Amongst the practicalities of 'Paid Liam £10', the 'Note re stud at Kildare' of 2 and 3 January 1922, his diaries were no place for the disquiet of his thoughts.[8] On 5 January Collins wrote to Kitty Kiernan 'this is the worst day I have had yet – far far the worst. May God help us all.'[9] His diary entry was 'Dail [sic] meetings During this period', nothing more.[10]

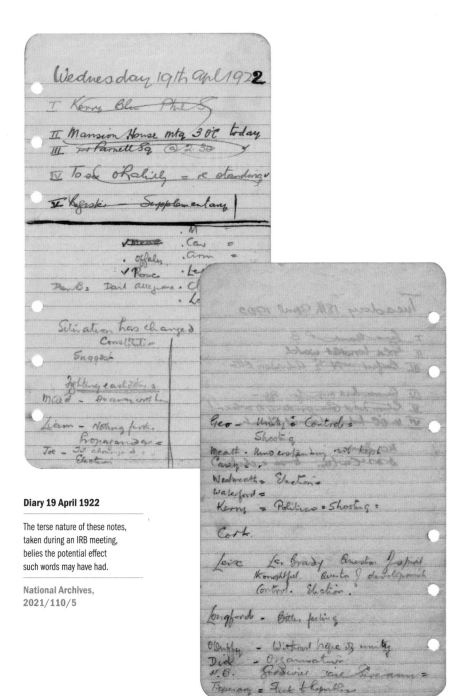

Diary 19 April 1922

The terse nature of these notes, taken during an IRB meeting, belies the potential effect such words may have had.

National Archives, 2021/110/5

The Treaty split has been understood as a moment of crisis, a rupture of something whole, the cause of civil war, but Collins's diaries don't allow us to make sense of it like that. Divisions were inherent in the cabinet he represented in London, and right across the War of Independence, alongside the common cause found, grievance had flourished and slights thrived. Just after the truce in July 1921 Collins wrote to Harry Boland that 'I find myself looking at friends as if they were enemies – looking at them twice just to make sure that they really are friends after all'.[11] The pressures of the negotiations, with Collins pulled between the expectations of home and the demands of London, can only have intensified that feeling. Although the Treaty certainly provoked acrimony in its own right, those for and against the agreement became adversaries not only because they had taken different sides. Sometimes they took different sides because they were already so very much at odds.[12] On 5 November 1921, having returned to Dublin to report on the negotiations' progress, Collins noted bluntly in his diary 'Stack & Brugha to bust it up'.[13] And he must have recorded 'Returned from Ireland' to London on 4 December 1921 with a very heavy heart.[14] Even before he signed the Treaty, Collins seemed to know that it was a question of how, not if, it would all come apart. As ever, he set to work among the wreckage.

His 1922 diary is a lesson in the pace of things. Those weeks and months from the vote on the Treaty on 7 January 1922 to the opening salvos of civil war at the end of June were long, longer than most histories of the period acknowledge. Each diary page after another slows those days right down with meetings, appointments, with longer and longer lists of things to do. But each of those same full pages shows the hurry and speed of the many different directions he was both going and being pulled in. On 16 January 1922 he went to meetings at 4.00, 5.00 and 8.00: the Provisional Government, the Dáil cabinet, and then the standing committee of Sinn Féin.[15] In those few hours alone came the imperative to establish the new Free State, the obligation of honouring commitments made in London, but also the expectation to bend the Treaty into the 'freedom to achieve' the freedom the Dáil and all shades in Sinn Féin desired.[16] Tom Barry was in his diary on the same day, so the IRA was also on his mind.[17]

Each day that followed was a version of the same struggle with incompatible positions. On 24 and 26 January he noted 'Beggars Bush' barracks.[18] On 30 January

you haven't written — but then
I may be hard on you —there
may be a real reason and if
I said anything — but then I
don't say anythings that I
have to regret afterwards.

Things are rapidly becoming
as bad as they can be and
the country has before it what
may be the ~~first~~ worst
period yet. A few madmen may
do anything. Indeed they are
just getting on the pressure gradually
— they go on from cutting a tree
to cutting a railway line, then
to firing at a barrack, then to
firing at a lorry, and so on.
But God knows I do not want

**Michael Collins
to Kitty Kiernan,
10 April 1922**

In this letter to Kitty
Kiernan he reflects on
how easily conflict will
escalate when it comes.
His sense of foreboding
is all the more striking
given the ordinary life she
continued to live through
during these days.

National Library of
Ireland, Ms 49,618

to be worrying you with these
things.
          Are you going to Nobber for
Easter? Or are you going anywhere
I'm most awfully anxious to see
you quickly and this week is
going to be a bad week with
me by the look of things. Any
improvement in the Connemara
plans yet? Kitty do please
hurry with making that definite
but I am anxious about you.
I wonder if you're writing even
today — yes? No?
          May God bless you
          Fondest love Micheal

he met General Macready at City Hall, and 'Genl McCready [sic]' again the next day.[19] He dealt with 'Sir John Anderson', and '11.30 Mr Cope', but then the very different demands of the 'Sinn Fein [sic] Ard Feis today'.[20] On the 31 March 1922 he wrote 'Question 1000 revolvers' and followed this on the next line with 'Make ap for meeting re Candidates'; revolvers and preparing for elections in the same breath.[21] His 'Guns Oriel House' reminds us of the methods he was ready to use.[22] His squad and his Department of Intelligence had to be managed; care had to be taken of his 'Special staff'.[23] As the months passed, he seemed to be running between so many spinning plates. 'Note to get truce extended' on 5 May was followed shortly by 'Note re Lloyd Geo[rge] Letter on Constitution'.[24] London was shocked by the draft constitution: 'my colleagues take a most grave view', Churchill wrote.[25] On 20 May he recorded, 'Subject to the Agreement arrived at between the M.[inister for] F[inance] & deputy de Valera & approved of by An Dáil an election is hereby declared for the Constituencies of—', his summary of the electoral pact made with de Valera, a pact which Churchill excoriated as the work of 'a tyrannical junta'.[26] Two days later Collins wrote 'Push Evacuation' of the British forces along with a particularly emphatic 'N.B.'.[27] He kept filling the diary's days, kept on pushing, but there was no distance left to run.

Once the guns were turned on the anti-Treaty forces in the Four Courts on 28 June, he took to civil war with the same purpose he brought to all his work. The next day he had an appointment in 'Portobello' barracks, and on 30 June it was all war:

'I 200 Mills
100 Rifle Grenades
200 H.[and?] G.[renades?]
II Speed up Arm[oured] Cars
III Return Portobello'.[28]

Although his notes of a meeting on 1 July with Archbishop of Dublin, Edward Byrne, the Lord Mayor of Dublin, Laurence O'Neill, and Labour's Cathal O'Shannon seemed conciliatory to the point of 'We don't want any humiliating surrender', he used the term 'irregulars' to describe the anti-Treatyites, and by 2 July he was writing about 'Stoke [sic] mortars'.[29] Ten days later he was made head of the 'Council of War'.[30] He set about war by work. He wanted lists of 'Commanders', of 'Telephone Nos of whole Barracks'; he wanted to know about

The Main Hall of the Four Courts, 1922

Collins was keen to examine the extent of the damage. He made
several notes in his diary about the Four Courts in July 1922,
and on 12 July 1922 recorded 'Return of mace (Four Courts)'.

National Library of Ireland, INDH248

'Commissions & Ranks & Uniforms'.[31] He had 'To work out Intelligence ideas &
objectives'; he wanted 'Instructions re Cipher & Cipher work'.[32] 'Telegraphists'
were needed, and a 'Good Surgeon with Portable X-Ray' machine was required.[33]
There was the 'Censorship of Country newspapers' to look after, the 'Question
of Petrol and prohibition', and he had to remember to 'advertise for Armourers
Mechanics'.[34] There were 'Routine orders' to 'Speak to McGann' about, and the
'Issue of Cartridges' to arrange; in civil war he was the busiest of men.[35]

From the beginning, he did reckon with the costs of this civil war. On 2
July he wrote 'Note re Four Courts & protection of Remains'.[36] He went with the
'Board of Works' to inspect the damage in a matter of days.[37] He measured the
costs in more than burning documents and bricks and mortar, but, in his diary,
in rather matter-of-fact ways. He made a note of 'Identification discs' on 3 August
as news of 'the splendid men we have lost on our side' in the Kerry landings came
through.[38] 'We have had a hard few days here', he wrote to Kitty in early August.
'The scenes at the Mass yesterday were really heartbreaking. The poor women
weeping and almost shrieking (some of them) for their dead sons'.[39] 'It makes
one feel I tell you', might well have been at the root of those 'Identification discs'.[40]

↑
'It means nothing to them' by 'Shemus',
Freeman's Journal, **26 April 1922**

Two days before the civil war began, this image by
'Shemus' was published in the *Freeman's Journal.*
Drawn from a pro-Treaty stance, it captures the ominous
feeling that nothing at that point could stop war.

National Library of Ireland, PD 4309 TX 118

→
**Members of the committee responsible
for drafting the constitution of
the Irish Free State, 1922**

National Library of Ireland, KEN2

'TAKING OVER GENERALLY'

'TAKING OVER GENERALLY'

After three plenary sessions of the negotiations in London, he thought of J.J. McElligott. Collins had been in the cell next to him in Stafford Gaol in 1916, and on 14 October 1921 he noted down McElligott's phone number at the financial magazine, *The Statist*, 'City 5258'.[1] From the moment he got to London money was on his mind, not as it had been in the 1919 or 1920 diaries, with all their gathering in and paying out, with their 'Lent Casey 10/=', with their reminders to pay the rent.[2] Now it was money of a different order: 'To read up Financial Costs' he wrote on 12 October, after one day of negotiations.[3] 'Wednesday next for Finance Cttee', he jotted down the following day.[4] After meeting McElligott on a Sunday morning, Collins seems to have considered asking him to take part in the 'Commission on Finance if necessary'. Though McElligott was not called upon for 'Wednesday next', the instinct to see him, to seek out his economic expertise, is a telling one at that point.[5] The big words of the revolution—freedom, republic, independence—could indulge all sorts of hopes. The imminent reality of a state, whatever its form, meant the lights had to be kept on.[6] It was coming time for plans to be borne out.

It wasn't that Collins was without plans until this point. It is more that his diaries were not necessarily the place he chose to expand upon them. He left hints though. One entry from November 1919 suggests his approach was a quite pragmatic one: 'Saw John C.[hartres]…Discussed question of Financial R[e]lations between England & Ireland. Land Purchase etc'.[7] On 22 February 1920 he 'Saw FS [?] & Mr B re Housing'.[8] The following day he was taken by a 'Local Gov[ernment] Mem[orandum]' on an 'Abolition of Poor Law Idea'.[9] He was in no doubt about the scale of these problems, but in 1919 and 1920 there were limits to what could be achieved beyond keeping going as an underground government. Which explains the different character the 1922 diary takes on: immediately, in January, he wanted 'Estimates', more 'Estimates', 'Estimates from MacMahon & Depts gen[era]ly', and 'Balances' to see just where he stood.[10] By 28 January he was taken up with the 'Question of Financial Returns', with a 'Note re Accountants Monday', even by the 'Question of Russian Trade Relations' all on the one day.[11] The following month it was the 'Repayment of Loans'.[12] On the day the National Army attacked the anti-Treaty forces in the Four Courts, it was 'Note re overdraft', but in those changed circumstances of civil war, it was also '£180,000 Defence'.[13]

Diary, 17 January 1922

Many of the names recorded here formed the committee which drafted the Free State constitution. Collins attended only the inaugural session and one other meeting but kept in regular contact with several members.

National Archives, 2021/110/5

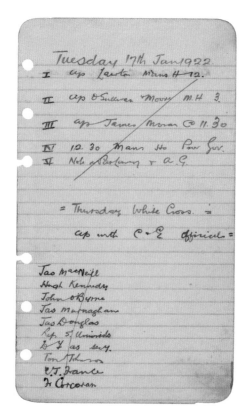

He was 'Taking over Generally' as he put it on 31 January, sizing up what was possible in the circumstances, what could be done.[14]

Names started to appear that confirmed this 'Taking over' had begun. On 20 April 1922, Diarmuid Fawsitt's name was noted.[15] Fawsitt was an IRB man; he had served as the Republic's consul-general in the United States and was brought to London with the Treaty delegation. By the time his name was written in the diary he was acting secretary to the Provisional Government's Department of Economic Affairs.[16] Most often came 'K. O'S' or Kevin O'Shiel.[17] A judicial commissioner of the Dáil Land Commission, O'Shiel was assistant legal advisor to the Provisional Government, and through March, April and May, he wrote variations of 'K O'S re Land Purchase', again and again.[18] The urgency of a land bill was not lost on Collins, and his diary refers regularly to the importance of the Irish 'Convention Land Purchase Report' of 1918.[19] It would later contribute to the shape of the 1923 Land Act. He made several references to the 'Nat[ional]

Land Bank', and he seemed particularly keen to meet with Department of Agriculture officials: 'Dept of Agriculture & Miceal Reidy', 'Willie Blundell Dept Agriculture – Re ap Ministry Finance'.[20] By July he was occupied by the 'Diseases of Animals Act'.[21] Michael Collins is not often associated with land and agricultural policy: his 1922 diary suggests we might reconsider that.

But it wasn't only land. 'Each separate Ministry Memo re Possible Conference', suggests every department came in for his intense scrutiny, and, again, the diaries hint at some of his plans.[22] 'Question Housing', 'Housing Scheme', 'Waterworks', 'Telegraphic System', 'Telephone [System]', 'Memo re Schools', 'Board of Trade Electricity Undertakings' are indicative of his concerns, and many of these issues were to be the focus of his plans for 'Educational Films' to concentrate 'the People's minds on the great problems of construction and retrenchment'.[23] His planned meeting with 'Dr Crowley of Siemins [sic]' in January 1922 may well have informed his proposal for a film on 'the great question of a national power generator'.[24] He wanted 'Pictures of what Northcliffe described as the "White Coal of Ireland". Hundreds of great Waterfalls all over the country going to waste.'[25] Maybe he has his place in the history of what became the Shannon Scheme.

Dr Crowley wasn't the only one who knew that Collins was the one worth seeing. 'Dismissed c[ivil]/s[ervants] @ 11', the 'French Consul', the 'Archbishop Dublin', and the 'Rep[resentative] Body Church [of] Ireland'.[26] He noted '4 O'C Sir Joseph Glynn', but whether he met Glynn in his capacity as chair of the Irish Insurance Commissioners or as president of the Society of Saint Vincent de Paul his diary is not clear.[27] These were just some who sought him out in January 1922. In 'Taking over Generally' he seemed to assume all sorts of responsibilities: 'met teachers with address for me', 'Labour Reps @ 11'.[28] As the man with most power, it was naturally assumed he could fix everything. As he travelled round the country making a case for the Treaty, he made notes of individuals' grievances and expectations, things he needed to remember and put right. 'Note re Crowley Ballylanders & P.O', seemed to be about John Crowley's claim that he had 'the charge of post office taken from me by British authorities', and John Crowley wanted his post office back.[29] 'Mr James McCarthy Main St Dunmanway C[omman] dant Kearney Two horses taken on Monday night 13th March = Boycott on him. Tans & his Daughter etc'; 'Taken ~~two~~ ^one^ cows': these were the workings out of new hierarchies and old scores.[30] In the days before the June election his constituents had his ear.

'Note re Young.
Xian [Christian] Bro[ther]s Schools
? Qualifications – Language
Dan Hurley. No Irish
Model School Morrison
- ? Ap re Principal'.[31]

It seems someone wasn't happy in Dunmanway with the giving out of teachers' jobs. Elections were always personal, even in June 1922.

Throughout these months, while he was making notes about 'Mrs Sugrue N.[ational] T.[eacher] Foynes' and looking for a 'Flat for Dan Breen', he was also marking out the character of the state.[32] Given his actions at the time, what he intended that character to be is still open to debate, and his diary does little to help us clarify his stance. On 17 January 1922 his diary recorded a list of names, the makings of the committee to draft the Free State constitution.[33] An attempt was made to draft an effectively republican constitution, amenable to the anti-Treaty forces, for this new Free State, but this was thwarted by the British government, which considered his actions at odds with the spirit of the Treaty. His diary gives no indication of what he hoped to achieve in the drafting process, nor any explanation of his stance on the electoral pact with de Valera in May 1922. If the democratic expression of the public will on the Treaty was to be sacrificed by that pact in the hope of averting civil war, he did not use the pages of his diary

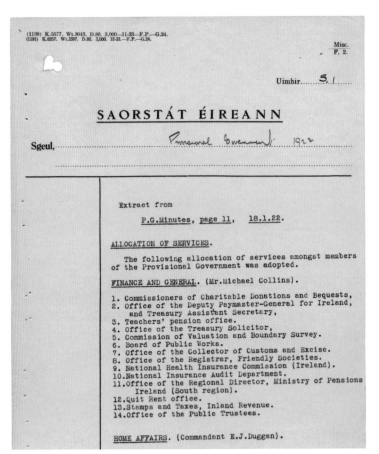

Misc.
F. 2.

Uimhir...... S. I

SAORSTÁT ÉIREANN

Sgeul, ... Provisional Government 1922 ....

Extract from

P.G.Minutes, page 11, 18.1.22.

ALLOCATION OF SERVICES.

The following allocation of services amongst members
of the Provisional Government was adopted.

FINANCE AND GENERAL. (Mr.Michael Collins).

1. Commissioners of Charitable Donations and Bequests,
2. Office of the Deputy Paymaster-General for Ireland,
   and Treasury Assistant Secretary,
3. Teachers' pension office.
4. Office of the Treasury Solicitor,
5. Commission of Valuation and Boundary Survey.
6. Board of Public Works.
7. Office of the Collector of Customs and Excise.
8. Office of the Registrar, Friendly Societies.
9. National Health Insurance Commission (Ireland).
10.National Insurance Audit Department.
11.Office of the Regional Director, Ministry of Pensions
   Ireland (South region).
12.Quit Rent office.
13.Stamps and Taxes, Inland Revenue.
14.Office of the Public Trustees.

HOME AFFAIRS. (Commandant E.J.Duggan).

List of the departments, commissions and offices Collins inherited responsibility for after the handover of Dublin Castle

The scale of this list is telling in terms of the very sudden expansion of Collins's role in January 1922.

National Archives, TAOIS/3/S1

to explain his choice. 'To decide re Meeting Dail [sic]' of 24 July 1922 was the only remark his diary made on postponing the meeting of the new parliament elected in June.[34] Similarly, his diary records only the public side of his Northern Ireland policy: 'Note re North opting out', 'Protest to all Govts re N.[orth] E.[ast]', 'Belfast & N.E. Advisory Cttee', 'Bishop Cleary & N.E. Atrocities'.[35] It was silent about the military activity he sanctioned along and across the border. His diary had never been the place for him to sift the rights out from the wrongs, and that certainly did not change in 1922.

On 16 January 1922 he wrote a short note to Kitty Kiernan: 'I am as happy a man as there is in Ireland today…Have just taken over Dublin Castle and am writing this note while awaiting a meeting of my Provisional Government. What do you think of that? Otherwise I see all sorts of difficulties ahead, but never mind.'[36] How the difficulties he faced measured up to the difficulties he foresaw, we may never know. 'But never mind', never mind.

RECEIVED
26 JAN. 1921
ANS⁰ ....

Eden Hotel,
Berlin.
21.1.22.

A chara dhil,

I have just been reading the accounts of the surrender of the Castle, & my mind recalls some conversations we had less than two years ago about that ill-famed fortress & certain possibilities of its early future. When I reflect upon the stupendous stride made since those talks in 1920 & also upon the astonishing appropriateness of the surrender into your own hands, I cannot help sending you

a word of warm personal congratulation. The flag will have to be carried, & I am sure will eventually be carried a little farther. Meanwhile the victory actually gained & the opportunities it offers for national recovery & consolidation are dazzling. I think I know something of the magnitude of your own contribution to what has been gained & the great inspiration it has been to others. I congratulate you again & wish you all

good fortune in your work for Ireland.

do chara go buan,

John Chartres

John Chartres, Berlin,
to Michael Collins,
21 February 1922

Chartres's letter captures
the sense of joy taken
in that moment that the
Castle was handed over.

National Archives,
TSCH/3/S9242

153

ENDNOTES

READING THE MICHAEL COLLINS DIARIES
1 Diary of Michael Collins (DMC), 6 Aug. 1922.

THE DIARIES
1 https://stors.tas.gov.au/download/CRO2-1-9 [accessed, 11 May 2022].
2 Joe Moran, 'Private lives, public histories: the diary in twentieth-century Britain', *Journal of British Studies* 54:1 (2015), 143–4; Anthony Letts, 'A history of Letts' in *Letts keep a diary: a history of diary keeping in Great Britain from 16ᵗʰ-20ᵗʰ century* (London, 1987), 31.

A DIARY-SHAPED LIFE
1 Peter Hart, *Mick: the real Michael Collins* (London, 2005), 250.
2 Diary of Michael Collins (DMC), 12 Jan. 1918; 20 Feb. 1918; 28 Mar 1918; 12, 21 May 1918; 9 Feb. 1918 'Céilide Mansion House at 8. 8 O'Clock no 41'.
3 Joseph E.A. Connell Jr, *Michael Collins: Dublin 1916–22* (Dublin, 2017).
4 DMC, 10 Sept. 1920.
5 References to Downing Street include 21 and 24 Oct. 1921. For House of Lords see entries for 27 Oct. 1921 and 6 Feb. 1922.
6 DMC, 8 Mar, 1922.
7 DMC, 1 Aug. 1922.
8 'Dr Barniville re Johnny Pain going from wrist to knuckles', DMC, 28 Apr. 1922.

ABSENCES
1 Harold Nicolson on 'the engagement book' diary, *Spectator*, 2 Jan. 1942.
2 DMC, 11 Feb. 1922. He also refers to an 'aps [appointments] Diary' on 10 Feb. 1922.
3 DMC, 5 Aug. 1922.
4 See, for example, *Irish Independent, Western People, Nenagh Guardian, Sligo Telegraph, Connaught Telegraph*, 5 Aug. 1922.
5 See Michael Collins to Kitty Kiernan, 2 and 4 Aug. 1922 (NLI, Ms 31,697(1)).
6 Piaras Béaslaí, *Michael Collins and the making of a new Ireland* (Dublin, 1926); David Neligan, *The spy in the castle* (London, 1968), Batt O'Connor, *With Michael Collins in the fight for Irish independence* (London, 1929).
7 'Mrs deV', DMC, 27 July 1918. Direct reference to 'Mrs de V' appear seven times to her husband's six, but there are also indirect references, such as to 'Fada Edward' on 15 March 1919, which may also refer to de Valera.
8 DMC, 17 May 1918.
9 DMC, 18 May 1918.
10 DMC, 11 Nov. 1918; 28 June 1919.
11 DMC, 9 May 1919.
12 DMC, 12 July 1922.
13 DMC, 29 June 1922.
14 Moran, 'Private lives, public histories', 158.

FAMILY
1 See, DMC, 10 Nov. 1918, 1 Dec. 1918, 8 Feb. 1919, 13 Apr. 1919, 11 May 1919, 6 July 1919. He also wrote on a bank holiday, 26 Aug. 1918.
2 Katty Hurley was married to Seán Collins. She died in 1921. Hart, *Mick*, 15.
3 DMC, 24 Feb. 1919 and 16 May 1919.
4 See, for example, DMC, 8 Nov. 1921, 6 Feb. 1922.
5 'P.J. Collins 7328 Blackstone Av Chic III', DMC, 1920, final page.
6 Memoir of Collins's time in London by Johanna Collins (NLI, Piaras Béaslaí papers, Ms 33,929(19)); *Westminster Gazette*, 25 Aug. 1922; Hart, *Mick*, 15.
7 DMC, 13 Apr. 1919. Helena Collins became Sister Mary Celestine in religious life.
8 Certificate of death for Mary Anne Collins, https://civilrecords. irishgenealogy.ie/churchrecords/images/deaths_returns/ deaths_1907/05526/4548863.pdf [accessed, 2 June 2022].
9 DMC, 16 Mar. 1918, 30 Mar.-1 Apr. 1918, 4–6 Jan. 1919, 14–17 Aug. 1919, 25–27 Dec. 1921, 16–18 Mar. 1922.
10 DMC, 4 Jan. 1919.
11 Hart, *Mick*, 15; Tim Pat Coogan, *Michael Collins: a biography* (London, 1990), 9 and 429. Brother and sister shared an affection for George Eliot's *The Mill on the Floss*.
12 DMC, 9 Nov. 1919.
13 Patrick Powell died on 4 Oct. 1919, Certificate of Death, https://civilrecords. irishgenealogy.ie/churchrecords/images/deaths_returns/ deaths_1919/05134/4413931.pdf [accessed, 2 June 2022].

14 Memoir by Mary Collins Powell, *c.*1950s (UCD Archives (UCDA), Seán MacEoin papers, P151/1851); Memo by W. Mandeville, 27 Mar. 1954 (Military Service Pension Collection (MSPC), DP23755); Report by D.E. Buckley, Social Welfare Officer, of a meeting with Mary Collins Powell, 10 Feb. 1954 (MSPC, DP23755). A diary entry in April 1920 recorded 'sent cheque £25 & £1 to Mary today', 8 Apr. 1920.
15 Award certificate, Mrs Mary Powell, 28 May 1954 (MSPC, DP23755).
16 DMC, 29 Jan. 1922.
17 Birth certificate of Mary Clare Powell, 22 Aug. 1907, https:// civilrecords.irishgenealogy.ie/churchrecords/images/ birth_returns/births_1907/01683/1669118.pdf [accessed, 2 June 2022].
18 DMC, 30 Aug. 1918, 12 Sept. 1918, 15, 24 July 1919, 16 Nov. 1919, 9 Apr. 1920, 15 Dec. 1921, 21, 31 Mar. 1922, 28 Apr. 1922, 16 May 1922.
19 DMC, 21 Mar. 1922. The same note was made on 31 Mar. 1922.
20 DMC, 28 Apr. 1922 and 16 May 1922.
21 *Sunday Independent*, 10 May 1964.
22 *Sunday Independent*, 10 May 1964.

'ELECTION EXCITEMENT'
1 DMC, 1 Dec. 1918.
2 See Lot 449, https://www.adams.ie/Independence/19-04- 2011?gridtype=listview&ipp=All&keyword=&lot_detail_ id=11785&low_estimate=0&page_no=1&sort_by=high_low_ hammer#11785 [accessed 19 June 2022].
3 DMC, 28 Nov. 1918.
4 Collins to Stack, 28 Nov. 1918 (NLI, Ms 5,848).
5 See Lot 449, https://www.adams.ie/Independence/19-04- 2011?gridtype=listview&ipp=All&keyword=&lot_detail_ id=11785&low_estimate=0&page_no=1&sort_by=high_low_ hammer#11785 [accessed 19 June 2022]. The 'Party' was the Irish Party, which had dominated Irish nationalist politics since the 1880s, promoting the objective of Home Rule for Ireland.
6 DMC, 1 Jan. 1918.
7 *Freeman's Journal*, 2 Jan. 1918. Even at this point, a peace conference at the end of the war was expected and featured in Sinn Féin's thinking.
8 Michael Laffan, *The Resurrection of Ireland: the Sinn Féin party 1916-1923* (Cambridge, 1999), 122–5.
9 *The Irish Times*, 2 Feb. 1918, as cited in Elaine Callinan, *Electioneering and propaganda in Ireland, 1917-21: votes, violence and victory* (Dublin, 2020), 170.
10 DMC, 18, 21, 23, 25, 29, 30, 31 Jan., and 1 and 2 Feb. 1918.
11 DMC, 8, 11, 13, 15 and 19 Mar. 1918.
12 DMC, 23 Mar. 1918.
13 See Laffan, *The Resurrection of Ireland*, 142–9, for introductions to both the German Plot and the East Cavan by-election.
14 DMC, 21 May 1918; Minutes of Sinn Féin Standing Committee (SFSC), 21 May 1918 (NLI, 3269).
15 DMC, 8 July 1918; Minutes of SFSC, 8 July 1918 (NLI, 3269).
16 Minutes of SFSC, 19 Sept. 1918 (NLI, 3269); *Irish Independent*, 20 Sept. 1918.
17 DMC, 30 Aug. 1918.
18 See Lot 449, https://www.adams.ie/Independence/19-04- 2011?gridtype=listview&ipp=All&keyword=&lot_detail_ id=11785&low_estimate=0&page_no=1&sort_by=high_low_ hammer#11785 [accessed 19 June 2022].

ASSOCIATION
1 R.V. Comerford, *The Fenians in context: Irish politics and society, 1848-82* (Dublin, 1985); Owen McGee, *The I.R.B.: the Irish Republican Brotherhood from Land League to Sinn Féin* (Dublin, 2005). M.J. Kelly, The Fenian ideal and Irish nationalism, 1882-1916 (Woodbridge, 2008).
2 DMC, 5 and 6 Mar. 1918.
3 *Irish Independent*, 6 Mar. 1918.
4 Death certificate of Mathew Murphy, https://civilrecords. irishgenealogy.ie/churchrecords/images/deaths_returns/ deaths_1918/05195/4435332.pdf [accessed 23 June 2022].

5 Gearoid Ua h-Uallachain, Witness Statement (MA, BMH, WS 328); Sean O Mahony, *Frongoch: university of revolution* (Dublin, 1987), 188; Military Service Pension Application, 23 Jan. 1935, http://mspcsearch. militaryarchives.ie/docs/files//PDF_Pensions/R2/ MSP34REF1301JohnMurphy/WMSP34REF1301JohnMurphy. pdf [accessed 23 June 2022].

6 For some examples see DMC, 6 Apr., 13 Sept., 10 Oct. and 8 Nov. 1919.

7 DMC, 24 Apr. 1919.

8 Joseph Furlong, Witness Statement (MA, BMH, WS 335); Seán Nunan, Witness Statement (MA, BMH, WS 1744).

9 DMC, 8 May 1919.

10 Eunan O'Halpin and Daithí Ó Corráin, *The Dead of the Irish revolution* (New Haven, 2020), 194.

11 Brenda Malone, 'The IRA "Big Gun" and the death of Matt Furlong, 1920', https://thecricketbatthatdiedforireland.com/tag/parnell-street/ [accessed 23 June 2022].

12 DMC, 15 Feb. 1919.

13 C.J. Woods, *Bodenstown revisited: the grave of Theobald Wolfe Tone, its monuments and its pilgrimages* (Dublin, 2018), 44.

14 León Ó Broin, *Revolutionary underground: the story of the Irish Republican Brotherhood 1858–1924* (Dublin, 1976), 91.

15 Woods, *Bodenstown revisited*, 90.

16 William Murphy, *Political imprisonment and the Irish, 1912–1921* (Oxford, 2014), 89.

17 DMC, 19 Apr. 1920.

18 DMC, 6 Jan. 1918.

19 Patrick Lawson, Witness Statement (MA, BMH, WS 667); Padraig Yeates, 'Michael Collins's "secret service unit" in the trade union movement', *History Ireland* 22:3 (May/June 2014), 42–3.

20 DMC, 14 June 1919.

21 DMC, 23 Jan. 1920 and 12 Nov. 1920.

22 Maryann Gialanella Valiulis, *Portrait of a revolutionary: General Richard Mulcahy and the founding of the Irish Free State* (Dublin, 1992), 27–8.

23 For examples see DMC, 26 June, and 5, 8, 17, 23 and 25 July.

24 For examples see DMC, 21 Feb., 28 Mar. and 25 Apr. 1918 ; Connell, *Michael Collins: Dublin 1916–22*, 78–9.

25 DMC, 20 and 27 June, 5, 6, 11 and 12 July, and 18 Aug. 1918.

26 *Enniscorthy Echo*, 14 and 21 Sept. 1918.

27 DMC, 21 Mar. and 9 Apr. 1920.

28 DMC, 21 July 1918.

29 DMC, 30 Jan. 1920.

30 Ed Vulliamy, 'My family's link to the 1916 Easter Rising', *Observer*, 27 Mar. 1916; https://kilmainhamgaolgraffiti.com/women-prisoners/ women-prisoners-womens-names-english/ [accessed, 1 July 2022]. See notes in frontmatter of DMC, 1918 and 1919.

31 Frank Thornton, Witness Statement (MA, BMH, WS 510).

32 DMC, 31 May and 1 June 1918.

'MURDERED BY THE ENGLISH TODAY'

1 There were only two brief entries for October 1920.

2 The entries for 1, 2 and 3 December were just the word 'away'. He noted his return on 13 December 1920.

3 DMC, 22 Nov. 1920. He made no reference to Conor Clune, the manager the Raheen Co-operative society, in Dublin to have the society accounts checked, who was arrested on 21 November, just a wrong man in the wrong place. Clune died with them in Dublin Castle. See O'Halpin & Ó Corráin, *The dead of the Irish revolution*, pp 232–3.

4 'Pierse McCann died in Gloucester this morning at 2.30', DMC, 6 Mar. 1919. He noted the funeral of Mattie Murphy in Mar 1918. DMC, 5 and 6 Mar. 1918. In a letter to his sister Hannie on 10 Nov. 1918 he wrote of the toll taken by influenza: 'Ever so many of my friends have died of it here – all and thro' the country. All sorts of great strong chaps & girls too.' See lot 448, https://www.adams.ie/Independence/19-04-2011?gridt ype=gridview&ipp=All&keyword=&lot_detail_id=11784&low_ estimate=0&page_no=1&sort_by=lot_no#11784 [accessed 30 June 2022].

5 'Requiem Mass @ Southwark Cathedral', DMC, 25 Oct. 1921.

6 McKee was also director of training on the general headquarters' staff. Marie Coleman, 'Dick McKee', *Dictionary of Irish biography* https://www.dib.ie/ biography/mckee-dick-richard-a5715 For details of Clancy see the claim for a dependant's allowance, MSPC, 1D412, http://mspcsearch. militaryarchives.ie/detail.aspx [accessed 18 May 2022].

7 For all the deaths of 21–22 November see O'Halpin & Ó Corráin, *The dead of the Irish revolution*, 222–34.

8 Quoted in Coogan, *Michael Collins*, 160.

9 See Hart, *Mick*, 110.

10 Richard Mulcahy, 'Conscription and the General Headquarters' staff', *The Capuchin Annual* (1968), 386.

11 Coogan, *Michael Collins*, 161.

12 DMC, 20 Nov. 1921. There were masses held throughout Dublin and newspapers estimated '10,000 Volunteers March to Glasnevin'. Collins was among those who laid a wreath on the graves. *Freeman's Journal*, 21 Nov. 1921. On 29 November 1921 he noted 'Paid £5 Dick McK wreath' in his diary.

KEEPING HIS SECRETS

1 Clare Sheridan, *In many places* (London, 1923), 28. Sheridan was a cousin of Winston Churchill and was in Ireland writing for the *New York World*.

2 DMC, 2–3 Mar. 1919; 28 Nov. 1919 (Full entry: 'Anything signed Michael Lalor will mean urgency, but no need to hire motor car provided bicycle good.').

3 DMC, 3 Dec. 1919; 15 July 1919.

4 DMC, 2 Mar. 1919; for example, 'Kildare v Wexford Replay Kildare fuair a buad.', DMC, 14 Mar. 1920.

5 Moran, 'Private lives, public histories', 154; DMC, 15 May 1918.

6 DMC, 9 Sept. 1918.

A TAXI FROM LINCOLN

1 DMC, 4 Feb. 1919. Éamon de Valera had been interned in May 1918 as part of the 'German Plot' round-up.

2 DMC, 18 Jan. 1919.

3 Bill Kelly, 'Escape of de Valera, McGarry and Milroy ('German Plot' prisoners) from Lincoln jail' in *IRA jailbreaks 1918-1921* (Dublin, 2010, reprint of 1971 edition), 52-69.

4 DMC, 19, 20 and 25 Jan. 1919.

5 Patrick O'Donoghue, Witness Statement (MA, BMH, WS 847). The Sir Thomas Beecham Opera Company were performing a season at the New Queen's Theatre and Opera House. See *Manchester Evening News*, 30 Jan. 1919.

6 Liam McMahon, Witness Statement (MA, BMH, WS 274)

7 DMC, 5 Feb. 1919.

8 Michael Lynch, Witness Statement (MA, BMH, WS 511).

PRISONERS

1 DMC, 28 Jan. 1922; *Cork Examiner*, 18 Apr. 1921, reveals they had refused to plea at the local petty sessions; Nos 397 and 398 (Dillon and Quane), General Register of Prisoners 1921, Clonmel General Register 1903–1925, Book 1/7/14.

2 DMC, 23 June 1922; No. 425 (Cornelius Shine), General Register of Prisoners 1921, Clonmel General Register 1903–1925, Book 1/7/14.

3 DMC, 5 Jan. 1918. The INA&VDF emerged from the amalgamation in August 1916 of the Irish National Aid Association (INAA) and the Irish Volunteer Dependents' Fund (IVDF). Both of these were founded in the aftermath of the Easter Rising with the purpose of supporting the dependents of those killed and imprisoned as well as the imprisoned themselves. At first, republicans drove the IVDF whereas the INAA drew in a wider constituency.

4 DMC, 2 Apr. 1918

5 DMC, 4 and 9 Jan.; 8 Feb.; 1, 4, 11 and 22 Mar. 1918.

6 DMC, 4 May 1918.

7 DMC, 2 Apr. 1918.

8 'Account in Michael Collins' hand of his capture and detention in Sligo Gaol, 2–21 April 1918', 54: https://catalogue.nli.ie/Record/ vtls000575484 [accessed 29 May 2022].

9 DMC, 4 and 10 Nov. 1918 and 15 Apr. 1919

10 DMC, 17 Mar. 1919.

11 Collins to Stack, 17 Mar. 1919 (Kilmainham Gaol Museum, 19LR-2225).
12 Robert Barton, Witness Statement (NAI, BMH, WS 979).
13 Diary of Michael Collins, 16 Mar. 1919.
14 Collins to Stack, 17 Mar. 1919 (Kilmainham Gaol Museum, 19LR-2225). Patrick O'Keeffe from Cork had been an internee at Usk when he won a seat at general election of December 1918.
15 DMC, 6 Mar. 1919.
16 DMC, 10 Mar. 1919. The authorities had released Kathleen Clarke a few weeks earlier, in mid-February, on medical grounds. Over the weeks that followed the papers regularly reported her ongoing ill-health. *Evening Herald*, 15 Feb. 1919; *Freeman's Journal*, 22 Feb. 1919; *Kerry News*, 3 Mar. 1919.
17 DMC, 15 Mar. 1919.
18 DMC, 6 Mar. 1919.
19 DMC, 8 Mar. 1919.
20 Initially, the IRPDF shared a headquarters with Sinn Féin. Leaving the consequences of the Easter Rising to the INA&VDF, it sought to support succeeding waves of prisoners and their dependents
21 For an example of a meeting, see DMC, 4 Mar. 1919. For examples of donations, see DMC, 18 and Mar., 22 May, 25 July, and 24 Dec. 1919.
22 DMC, 24 Nov. 1919 and 14 Apr. 1920.
23 For instance, the first meeting of that body saw the establishment of joint inspections of prisons and camps in Ireland. Committee on the Observance of the Truce, 12 Oct. 1921 (NAI, DE/2/304/1/10).
24 DMC, 17 Oct. and 1 and 12 Nov. 1921
25 DMC, 18 Oct. and 7 Nov. 1921.
26 DMC, 7 July 1922.
27 O'Keeffe was appointed on 13 July 1922. See application for military service pension by Pádraig O'Caoimh, 23 Feb. 1925, http://mspcsearch.militaryarchives.ie/docs/files// PDF_Pensions/R2/24SP8333PATRICKO'KEEFFE/ W24SP8333PATRICKO'KEEFFE.pdf [accessed 31 May 2022]; DMC, 16, 18, and 27 July 1922

PRIVATE LIVES

1 DMC, 10 May 1919.
2 'Account in Michael Collins' hand of his capture and detention in Sligo Gaol, 2–21 April 1918', 31: https://catalogue.nli.ie/Record/ vtls000575484 [accessed 5 June 2022]; Helen Kiernan married Paul McGovern, a solicitor from Enniskillen, on 5 October 1921, registration of marriage, https://civilrecords.irishgenealogy.ie/churchrecords/ images/marriage_returns/marriages_1921/09242/5345191. pdf [accessed 5 June 2022]. Frank O'Connor maintained that he 'pleaded with her not to go through with the marriage' on the night before her wedding and was 'so agitated the he shredded his handkerchief' during the wedding. See Chrissy Osbourne, *Michael Collins himself* (Cork, 2003), 68. Harry Boland referred to Helen as 'the Parisian Rose' in a letter to Kitty Kiernan, 9 Oct. 1919, quoted in David Fitzpatrick, *Harry Boland's Irish revolution* (Cork, 2003), 164.
3 Moya Llewellyn Davies was the daughter of a nationalist MP and the wife of Crompton Llewellyn Davies, solicitor general to the British post office. Radicalised by the Rising, she came to live in Dublin with her children in early 1920, and stored guns and gathered information for Collins. She later claimed to have been Collins's mistress. Lady Hazel Lavery was the wife of the painter Sir John Lavery. Referred to by Peter Hart as a 'social spider', her home was a place where delegates from both sides of the Treaty negotiations could meet. Her friendships often received the attention of 'professional gossips'. See Hart, *Mick*, 351. For a fuller exploration of the relationship between Collins and Lady Lavery see Sinéad McCoole, *Hazel: a life of Lady Lavery, 1880–1935* (Dublin, 1996), 63–108.
4 DMC, 1 Dec. 1921. Entries such as 'Ring up M. LD Park 2584' appeared on 31 Oct. 1921, 1 Nov. 1921, 7 Nov. 1921, 8 Nov. 1921, however he often repeated items in his diary from one day to the next when the task had not been done. 'Note ap[pointment] M.L.D @ 7 to 7.30' appeared on 9 Nov. 1921. Her phone number appears along with the details of the trip to the ballet and a meeting at Sloane Square Tube station on 17 Nov. 1921. The last entry about her was on 26 Jan. 1922 to note a phone

number: 'M.L.D Clontarf 40'.
5 Sir John Lavery was painting Collins's portrait along with portraits of the other delegates. He appears in the diary on 13, 15, 16 Nov. 1921, 21 Jan. 1922. A phone call to the Laverys was noted on 15 Feb. 1922. 'Re photo from Portrait. Photo for Lady Lavery' on 27 Nov. 1921 is the first mention of Hazel Lavery. She appears again on 16 Feb. 1922, 29 Mar. 1922, and the last reference was 13 June 1922.
6 George Bernard Shaw to Hazel Lavery, 7 Oct. 1922, quoted in McCoole, *Hazel*, 102.
7 DMC, 1 Feb. 1922.
8 DMC, 13 June 1922 and 9 Nov. 1921.
9 DMC, 15 Jan. 1922.
10 Michael Collins to Kitty Kiernan, 5 and 6 Dec. 1921, 21 Jan. 1922 (NLI, León Ó Broin papers, Ms 31,697(2)); Michael Collins to Kitty Kiernan, 23 Oct. 1921 (NLI, León Ó Broin papers, Ms 31,697(1)).
11 DMC, 13 May 1922, 23 Dec. 1921. The gold watch appears repeatedly in entries across January, Mar, April and May 1922. This might suggest he kept forgetting to get it done.
12 DMC, 12 June 1922.
13 DMC, 15 May 1922. After a trip to Granard he made a note to cancel an appointment with Farnan on 1 May 1922 and wrote to phone Farnan for a new appointment for her on 3 May 1922.
14 See *Irish Press*, 8 Jan. 1962; Colonel Eamon Broy, Witness Statement (MA, BMH, WS 1280); Síobhra Aiken, *Spiritual wounds: trauma, testimony and the Irish civil war* (Newbridge, 2022), 72 and 202.
15 Michael Collins to Dr Farnan, 23 Oct. 1921 in León Ó Broin (ed.), *In great haste: the letters of Michael Collins and Kitty Kiernan*, revised and extended by Cian Ó hÉigeartaigh (Dublin, 1996), 50.
16 Michael Collins to Kitty Kiernan, 24 Oct. 1921, in Ó Broin (ed.), *In great haste*, 52.
17 Ó Broin (ed.), *In great haste*, 1 Jan. 1919.

THE GAA

1 DMC, 6 Apr. 1919.
2 Another candidate is Luke Kennedy, centre of the Edward Walsh Literary and Debating Society (an IRB circle) and member of the Supreme Council of the IRB.
3 *Evening Herald*, 5 Apr. 1919; *Irish Independent*, 7 Apr. 1919.
4 Collins to Austin Stack, 26 Mar. 1919 (NLI, Ms 17,090). For a discussion of contradictory accounts of this debate see David Fitzpatrick, *Harry Boland's Irish Revolution* (Cork, 2003), 119 and 364.
5 *Irish Independent*, 7 Apr. 1919.
6 DMC, 6 Apr. 1919.
7 DMC, 9 Feb. 1919; *Cork Examiner*, 10 Feb. 1919.
8 For an interesting discussion of the relationship of the GAA to both the INA&VDF and the IRPDF see Mark Reynolds, 'The GAA and Irish Political Prisoners, 1916–23' in Gearóid Ó Tuathaigh (ed.), *The GAA & revolution in Ireland 1913–1923* (Cork, 2015), 186–7.
9 DMC, 13 Aug. 1919.
10 DMC, 18 Aug. 1918.
11 DMC, 31 Aug. 1919.
12 DMC, 28 July and 22 Aug. 1919.
13 DMC, 19 Oct. 1921.
14 DMC, 18 Dec. 1919.
15 DMC, 10 Mar. 1918, 3 Mar. 1919 and 5 Nov. 1921.
16 DMC, 2 July 1918, 27 Feb. 1919 and 25 May 1922.
17 DMC, 23 Feb. 1919; *Irish Independent*, 24 Feb. 1919.
18 DMC, 24 and 31 Aug., and 7 and 28 Sept. 1919.
19 *Cork Examiner*, 29 Sept. 1919.

THE MONEY

1 DMC, 27 Feb., 4 Mar., 22 May, and 24 Dec. 1919.
2 Collins to O'Brien, 19 May 1919 (NLI, Art O'Brien Papers, Ms 8429/11).
3 DMC, 6, 8, and 15 May 1919.
4 *Irishman*, 8 Feb. 1919.
5 DMC, 27 Mar. 1919. Richard Bowden had worked with him at the INA&VDF.
6 Poster (NAI, DE/2/530).

7   DMC, 27 Mar. and 27 Apr. 1919.

8   *Nationality*, 3, 17, 24 May 1919.

9   Patrick O'Sullivan Greene, *Crowdfunding the revolution: the first Dáil loan and the battle for Irish independence* (Dublin, 2020), 184. Examples of donations to the Self-Determination Fund are to be found in DMC, 11 Mar., 13 Apr., and 19 May 1920.

10 DMC, 9 May 1919.

11 *Dáil Éireann Debates*, 9 May 1919, Vol. F, No.8, cols 89–96, https://debatesarchive.oireachtas.ie/debates%20authoring/debateswebpack.nsf/takes/dail1919050900005?opendocument [accessed 28 June 2022].

12 O'Sullivan Greene, *Crowdfunding the revolution*; Francis M. Carroll, *Money for Ireland: finance, diplomacy, politics and the first Dáil Éireann loans, 1919–1936* (Westport, 2002).

13 DMC, 25 Oct. 1919.

14 DMC, 2 and 3 Feb. 1920; Collins to MacSwiney, 2 and 4 Feb. 1920 (NAI, DE/2/530).

15 DMC, 20 Apr. 1920.

16 The shorthand 'D.O'D' appears 21 times in the diaries during the first half of 1920. Less frequently, Collins wrote 'to Daithi'. For an example of both see DMC, 9 Jan. 1920.

17 O'Sullivan Greene, *Crowdfunding the revolution*, 187.

CLERGY

1   DMC, 18 May 1920.

2   DMC, 17 Jan, 8 and 12 May, 7, 24 and 25 June, and 6 Aug. 1920.

3   Laffan, *The resurrection of Ireland*, 199.

4   Brian Heffernan, *Freedom and the fifth commandment: Catholic priests and political violence in Ireland, 1919-21* (Manchester, 2014), 244 and 24.

5   Brian Heffernan, *Catholic priests and political violence in Ireland, 1919–21* (PhD, NUI Maynooth, 2011), 369–71. Brennan attended banned meetings frequently and presided at a Sinn Féin court. In July 1920, the police fired into his house. See Heffernan, *Freedom and the fifth commandment*, 102, 106, 118, and 191.

6   David W. Miller, *Church, state and nation in Ireland, 1898-1921* (Dublin, 1973), 412.

7   Jérôme aan de Wiel, *The Catholic church in Ireland 1914-1918: war and politics* (Dublin, 2003), 104; Heffernan, *Catholic priests and political violence*, 400. Michael Hayes, from Bruree, was a brother of Dr Richard Hayes, 1916 veteran and member of the Sinn Féin executive.

8   Heffernan, *Freedom and the fifth commandment*, 102.

9   Heffernan, *Freedom and the fifth commandment*, 188–9.

10 *Irish Catholic Directory 1920* (Dublin, 1920), 297.

11 See correspondence between Burke and Collins (UCDA, Papers of Margaret and Fr Tom Burke, IE UCDAD, P30).

12 *Irish Catholic Directory 1920* (Dublin, 1920), 143.

13 *Meath Chronicle*, 22 June 1918.

'WORKED ALL DAY CLEARED ALL ARREARS'

1   Report by the Royal Irish Constabulary of Michael Collins's arrival at Woodfield, 31 Dec. 1916 (The National Archives (TNA), CO904/196/65); 'Latest description' of Michael Collins from 'Castle File, No. 10', 4 June 1921 (TNA, WO35/206/35). The report was dated 4 June 1921, but the description originated in October 1920.

2   *Sunday Pictorial*, 27 Aug. 1922.

3   DMC, 4 Dec. 1921; 20 May 1922; 25 May 1922; Collins to Messrs Callaghan & Son, Ltd, Dame Street, Dublin, 5 Aug. 1922 (NLI, Piaras Béaslaí papers, Ms 33,929(15)). The American journalist, Hayden Talbot, produced his book, *Michael Collins' own story told to Hayden Talbot* (London 1923), from such meetings.

4   DMC, 27 Dec. 1921; 18 Mar. 1922; 21 Mar. 1918; 6 Jan. 1919.

5   DMC, 15 Oct. 1921.

6   DMC, 3–4 and 13–14 Jan. 1922.

7   DMC, 24 and 25 Feb. 1922.

8   DMC, 26 Feb. 1922.

9   DMC, 6 June 1922.

10 In his letters to Kitty Kiernan he mentions trouble sleeping regularly. See Ó Broin (ed.), *In great haste*; Hart, *Mick*, 264.

11 DMC, 9 and 10 Jan. 1919. There was another reference to the dentist on 9 May 1922.

12 DMC, 14 Apr. 1919.

THE 'BIG FELLA' AT THE BALLET

1   DMC, 1 Jan. 1918; *Freeman's Journal*, 2 Jan. 1918.

2   DMC, 6 Aug. 1922.

3   DMC, 2 Feb. 1918 and 9 Feb. 1918.

4   DMC, 4 June 1919. Paul Dawson Cusack married Violet Davis. Both were from Granard, and Cusack was a cousin of Kitty Kiernan. Fitzpatrick, *Harry Boland's Irish revolution*, 116. See marriage certificate at https://civilrecords.irishgenealogy.ie/churchrecords/images/marriage_returns/marriages_1919/09675/5508843.pdf [accessed on 21 May 2022].

5   DMC, 15 May 1922; *Evening Herald*, 15 May 1922; *Irish Independent*, 16 May 1922. This was the first time a pope had given permission for the Vatican choir to perform outside the pontiff's presence. After performing at the Albert Hall in London, the choir arrived for two performances in Dublin and was greeted at Dún Laoghaire by Minister for Local Government, W.T. Cosgrave, amongst others.

6   A phrase used by the travel writer, H.V. Morton, to describe the urgency to be seen with Collins in late 1921 and into 1922. H.V. Morton, *In search of Ireland* (London, 2000; 1st edn 1930), 21.

7   *Irish Independent*, 16 May 1922.

8   John Gibney & Zoë Reid (eds), *The Treaty 1921: records from the archives* (Dublin, 2022), 125.

9   DMC, 17 Nov. 1921; Signed programme for 'The beggar's opera' 27 Oct. 1921 (NLI, Michael Collins Jr papers, Ms 40,432/2).

10 P.S. O'Hegarty, *The victory of Sinn Féin* (Dublin, 1998; 1st edn 1924), 15; Joanna (Hannie) Collins to Piaras Béaslaí, 25 Sept. 1923 (NLI, Piaras Béaslaí papers, Ms 33,929(19)); Coogan, *Michael Collins*, 17–18.

11 DMC, 17 Nov. 1921; Signed programme for 'The beggar's opera', 27 Oct. 1921 (NLI, Michael Collins Jr papers, Ms 40,432/2). 'The sleeping princess' ran for 115 performances at the Alhambra Theatre. Described as a 'gorgeous calamity', the production costs led to legal action. https://www.loc.gov/item/ihas.200185235/ Running for more than 1,400 performances at the Lyric Theatre, 'The beggar's opera' broke theatrical records across 1920–23. https://www.bl.uk/collection-items/1921-edition-of-the-beggars-opera-illustrated-by-claud-lovat-fraser [accessed, 21 May 2022].

12 DMC, 5 Jan. 1918; 'The whiteheaded boy '1918 production, Abbey Theatre Archive, https://www.abbeytheatre.ie/archives/production_detail/993/; Tom Feeney, 'Arthur Shields', *Dictionary of Irish biography* https://www.dib.ie/biography/shields-arthur-a8055 [accessed 21 May 2022].

13 Joanna (Hannie) Collins to Piaras Béaslaí, 25 Sept. 1923 (NLI, Piaras Béaslaí papers, Ms 33,929(19)); Frank O'Connor, *The big fellow* (Dublin, 1996; 1st edn 1937), 22–3; DMC, 9 and 14 Jan. 1918, 1 July 1919; 'Call at Hodges Figges [sic]', 18 Jan. 1918.

14 DMC, 2 Mar. 1922, 'Catalogue Castle Library'.

15 O'Connor, *The big fellow*, 22–3.

LONDON

1   Michael Collins to Kitty Kiernan, 3 Dec. 1921 (NLI, León Ó Broin papers, Ms 31,697(2)).

2   DMC, 12 Oct. 1921; 13 Oct. 1921; 21 Jan. 1922; 27 Oct. 1921; 2 Nov. 1921; 14 Oct. 1921; 21 Jan. 1922; 30 Oct. 1921; 6 Feb. 1922; 17, 20, 21, 24, 30 Oct. 1921 and 6 Feb. 1922.

3   DMC, 2 Nov. 1921; 13 Oct. 1921; 13 June 1922; 27 Oct. 1921. 'Lloyd Geo.' and 'Lloyd G' referred to the Prime Minister, David Lloyd George; 'Chamb' was Austen Chamberlain, leader of the Conservative Party, leader of the House of Commons, and Lord Privy Seal; 'Lord B.' and 'Birk' referred to F.E. Smith, Lord Birkenhead, then Lord Chancellor. Beatty was David Beatty, Lord Beatty, First Sea Lord; 'Churchill' was Winston Churchill, then Secretary of State for the Colonies; 'Evans' was Laming Worthington-Evans, Secretary of State for War; 'Chetwood' was possibly Philip Walhouse Chetwode, 1st Baron Chetwode, Military Secretary to the Secretary of State for War and Deputy Chief of the Imperial General Staff.

4   *Manchester Guardian*, 24 Aug. 1922; Michael Collins's account of his

response to de Valera about being chosen as one of the negotiators, quoted in Hayden Talbot, *Michael Collins' own story* (Dublin, 2012; 1st edn. 1923), 106.

5 Michael Collins to Kitty Kiernan, no date (NLI, León Ó Broin papers, Ms 31,697(1)).

6 Michael Collins to Kitty Kiernan, 16 Nov. 1921 (NLI, León Ó Broin papers, Ms 31, 697(2)); DMC 17 Nov. 1921.

7 DMC, 26 Nov. 1921.

8 Michael Collins to Kitty Kiernan, 16 Nov. 1921 (NLI, León Ó Broin papers, Ms 31, 697(2)); John's painting of T.E. Lawrence of 1919 was presented to the Tate Gallery in 1920 by the Duke of Westminster, see https://www.tate.org.uk/art/artworks/john-colonel-t-e-lawrence-n03566 [accessed 10 June 2022]; see Béaslaí, *Michael Collins*, 299; McCoole, *Hazel*, 74.

9 DMC, 14 Oct. 1921. The last reference to Barrie was on 15 Feb. 1922.

10 John Lavery, *The life of a painter* (London, 1940), 165; McCoole, *Hazel*, 76; DMC, 19 Oct. 1921; 1 Nov. 1921; 14 Oct. 1921; 3 Nov. 1921; 9 Nov. 1921.

11 Coogan, *Michael Collins*, 18. Coogan also mentions the suspicion Barrie was held in by some anti-Treatyites. Because Barrie had been 'in Intelligence during the war', he was thought to be part of a British plot. Coogan, *Michael Collins*, 109.

12 Sean O'Hegarty, Officer Commanding Cork No. 1 Brigade, to Liam Lynch, Officer Commanding the 1st Southern Division, 22 Nov. 1921, quoted in Coogan, *Michael Collins*, 287.

13 See Frank Pakenham, *Peace by ordeal* (London, 1935); Gibney & Reid (eds), *The Treaty 1921*.

14 DMC, 20 Oct. 1921; 17 Oct. 1921; 24 Oct. 1921.

15 DMC, 24 Oct. 1921; 4 Nov. 1921; 16 Nov. 1921; 2 Dec. 1921.

16 DMC, 13 Oct. 1921.

17 DMC, 27 Oct. 1921.

18 Michael Collins to Kitty Kiernan, 8 Nov. 1921 (NLI, León Ó Broin papers, Ms 31, 697(2)); Michael Collins to Éamon de Valera, 12 Oct. 1921 quoted in Gibney & Reid (eds), *The Treaty*, 80.

19 DMC, 23 Nov. 1921.

20 Arthur Griffith to Maud Griffith, 22 Nov. 1921 (NLI, Arthur Griffith papers, Ms 49,530/8/3).

21 DMC, 15, 19 and 24 Oct. 1921; 3 Nov. 1921; 20 and 21 Oct. 1921. On Frank Fitzgerald see Gerard Noonan, *The IRA in Britain, 1919-1923* (Liverpool, 2014), 255-6.

22 DMC, 17 Oct. 1921.

23 William O'Keeffe, Witness Statement (MA, BMH, WS 1678). O'Keeffe refers to the Cullinane family, while the 1921 census records a 'Culliman' family instead.

24 Keith Jeffery, *Field Marshal Sir Henry Wilson: a political soldier* (Oxford, 2006); Ronan McGreevy, *Great hatred: the assassination of Field Marshal Sir Henry Wilson MP* (London, 2022).

25 DMC, 6 Feb. 1922. Argyll Road may refer to 52 Argyll Road, as this is mentioned as 'C's address 52 Argyll Road' in the diary entry for 16 Oct. 1921. According to the 1921 census, 52 Argyll Road was the home of the Kay family. Leah Kay married Cecil L'Estrange Malone in 1921. Malone was the Communist Party of Great Britain's first MP. Malone, a relative of Countess Markievicz, had been arrested in Dublin in November 1920 after delivering a speech to the Trinity College Dublin's History Society on Bolshevism. Of course, 'Argyll Road' may signify something else. On Malone, see Ray Wilson & Ian Adams, *Special branch: a history 1883-2006* (Hull, 2015).

26 DMC, 6 Feb. 1922; 'Statement by Eamon Duggan on reading Roger Casement's "Black Diary" with Michael Collins', no date (NLI, Joseph McGarrity papers, Ms 17,601/6/1); Deirdre McMahon, 'Roger Casement: an account from the archives of his reinterment in Ireland', *Irish Archives* (Spring 1996).

27 Churchill wrote to Collins with these views before the pact with de Valera was agreed. Winston Churchill to Michael Collins, 15 May 1922, quoted in Coogan, *Michael Collins*, 323; David Lloyd George, 27 May 1922, from 'Conference on Ireland with Irish ministers: meetings' (TNA, CAB21/249), quoted in Coogan, *Michael Collins*, 326.

28 From diary entries and letters to Kitty Kiernan he was in London on 21-22 Jan. 1922, 5-6 Feb. 1922, 15-16 Feb. 1922, 29-31 Mar. 1922, 26 May-1 June 1922, 12-13 June 1922.

29 Michael Collins to Kitty Kiernan, 29 Mar. 1922, 31 Mar. 1922, 28 May 1922, 31 May 1922, Ó Broin (ed.), *In great haste*, 150, 151, 175, 178.

THE TRUCE

1 DMC, 12 Oct. 1921.

2 Minute of Committee on the Observance of the Truce, 12 Oct. 1921 (NAI, Dáil Éireann Papers, DE/2/304/1/10).

3 Michael Hopkinson (ed.), *The last days of Dublin Castle: the diaries of Mark Sturgis* (Dublin, 1999), 219.

4 DMC, 17 Oct. 1921.

5 Thomas Jones, *Whitehall diary: volume III*, edited by Keith Middlemas (London, 1971), 132-4.

6 Report to Dáil Éireann from the Irish Delegation of Plenipotentiaries (NAI, Dáil Éireann Papers, DE/4/5/11).

7 Ronan Fanning, *Fatal path: British government and Irish revolution 1910-1922* (London, 2013), 288-96.

8 Collins to de Valera, 12 Nov. 1921 (NAI, Dáil Éireann Papers, DE/2/304/6/3).

9 DMC, 1 Nov. 1921.

10 Minute of Committee on the Observance of the Truce, 1 Nov. 1921 (NAI, Dáil Éireann Papers, DE/2/304/1/45).

11 *Nationalist and Leinster Times*, 5 Nov. 1921.

12 O'Halpin and Ó Corráin, *The dead of the Irish revolution*, 454-55 and 645.

13 DMC, 5 Nov. 1921.

14 Diarmuid O'Hegarty's handwritten notes of meeting of 4 Nov. 1921 (NAI, Dáil Éireann Papers, DE/2/304/6/4).

15 Minute of Committee on the Observance of the Truce, 4 Nov. 1921 (NAI, Dáil Éireann Papers, DE/2/304/1/42).

16 Richard Mulcahy to Collins, 10 Nov. 1921 (MA, Truce Liaison and Evacuation Papers, IE-MA-LE-29).

17 Mulcahy to Cathal Brugha, unclear but likely 2 Nov. 1921 (MA, Truce Liaison and Evacuation Papers, IE-MA-LE-29).

18 *Irish Independent*, 26 Nov. 1921.

19 For interesting reflections on arson see Gemma Clark, *Everyday violence in the Irish civil war* (Cambridge, 2014), 54-97.

20 DMC, 7, 12 and 29 Nov. 1921.

COMING TOGETHER, COMING APART

1 DMC, 27 Feb. 1919.

2 Sam Davies, '"A stormy political career": P.J. Kelly and Irish nationalist and labour politics in Liverpool, 1891-1936', *Journal of the Historic Society of Lancashire and Chesire*, 148 (1998), 147-89.

3 Mary MacDiarmada, *Art O'Brien and Irish nationalism in London, 1900-1925* (Dublin, 2020), 88.

4 For a short while, they edited the Gaelic League newspaper together. See MacDiarmada, *Art O'Brien*, 36-7.

5 MacDiarmada, *Art O'Brien*, 82-3.

6 Pádraig Manning, 'A mixing of social and national aspirations: the Irish Self-Determination League of Great Britain (ISDL), 1919-31', *History Ireland*, 27:6 (Nov./Dec. 2019), 42.

7 DMC, 24 Apr., 10 May, 22 Oct. and 20 Nov. 1919.

8 DMC, 13 June 1919. For more on the IRA in Britain see Noonan, *The IRA in Britain*.

9 DMC, 15 Nov. 1921; Diary of Art O'Brien, 15 Nov. 1921 (NLI, Art O'Brien Papers, Ms 8457/7).

10 Diary of Art O'Brien, 14 June 1922 (NLI, Art O'Brien Papers, Ms 8457/7).

11 MacDiarmada, *Art O'Brien*, 152-65.

12 Collins to O'Brien, 2 Mar. 1922 and O'Brien to Collins, 6 Mar. 1922 (NLI, Art O'Brien Papers, Ms 8425/11).

13 DMC, 8 May 1922.

WITHOUT HOPE OF UNITY

1 Lar Brady, IRB Leix, recalled this meeting in March 1922 in his interview with Ernie O'Malley on 21 Oct. 1950 (UCDA, Ernie O'Malley notebooks, P17B/116). Brady also attended the meeting of the IRB on 19 April 1922.

2 DMC, 18-19 Apr. 1922.

3 DMC, 18-19 Apr. 1922.

4 DMC, 18-19 Apr. 1922. Rex Taylor published these notes made by Collins in his biography, notes which were transcribed by Florence O'Donoghue. Gerard Murphy argues these notes made by Collins shows how openly

'doing away' with Collins was being discussed. Gerard Murphy, *The great cover-up: the truth about the death of Michael Collins* (Cork, 2018), chapter 8.

5   *Dáil Éireann official report: debate on the Treaty*, 7 Jan. 1922, 326.

6   DMC, 2 July 1922.

7   DMC, 14 Dec. 1921; 17 Dec. 1921; 21 Dec. 1921. Stockley made reference in the debates on 21 December to the Confederation of South German States prior to 1870 to disparage the oath in the Treaty. Although the Emperor of Austria was head of the Confederation no one in Bavaria had to swear allegiance to him. *Freeman's Journal*, 22 Dec. 1921. For detail on Stockley see Lawrence White, 'Professor Frederick Paul Stockley', *Dictionary of Irish biography* https://www.dib.ie/biography/stockley-william-frederick-paul-a8321 [accessed 22 June 2022].

8   DMC, 2 Jan. 1922; 3 Jan. 1922.

9   *Dáil Éireann official report: debate on the Treaty*, Séamus Robinson, 6 Jan. 1922; Michael Collins to Kitty Kiernan, 5 Jan. 1922, Ó Broin (ed.), *In great haste*, 102.

10 DMC, 5 Jan. 1922.

11 Michael Collins to Harry Boland, July 1921, quoted in Coogan, *Michael Collins*, 232.

12 Stathis N. Kalyvas, 'The ontology of "political violence": action and identity in civil wars', *Perspectives on Politics*, i, 3 (Sept. 2003), 479.

13 DMC, 5 Nov. 1921.

14 DMC, 4 Dec. 1921.

15 DMC, 16 Jan. 1922.

16 *Dáil Éireann official report: debate on the Treaty*, Michael Collins, 19 Dec. 1921.

17 DMC, 16 Jan. 1922.

18 DMC, 24 Jan. 1922; 26 Jan. 1922.

19 DMC, 30 Jan. 1922; 31 Jan. 1922. Sir Nevil Macready was general officer commanding the British forces in Ireland.

20 DMC, 1 Feb. 1922; 2 Feb. 1922; 21 Feb. 1922. John Anderson, 1st Viscount Waverley, and Alfred Cope, were two of the most significant civil servants in the Dublin Castle administration. See Patrick Maume, 'John Anderson', *Dictionary of Irish biography*, https://www.dib.ie/biography/anderson-john-a0153 and Richard Hawkins & Pauric J. Dempsey, 'Sir Alfred Cope', *Dictionary of Irish biography*, https://www.dib.ie/biography/cope-sir-alfred-william-andy-a2028 [accessed 22 June 2022].

21 DMC, 31 Mar. 1922.

22 DMC, 31 Mar. 1922.

23 DMC, 4 Feb. 1922.

24 DMC, 5 May 1922; 19 May 1922.

25 Winston Churchill to Hazel Lavery, quoted in Coogan, *Michael Collins*, 326.

26 DMC, 20 May 1922; Winston Churchill to Michael Collins, 15 May 1922, quoted in Coogan, *Michael Collins*, 323.

27 DMC, 22 May 1922.

28 DMC, 30 June 1922.

29 DMC, 1 July 1922; 2 July 1922. Stokes mortars were used by the British army in the Great War.

30 DMC, 12 July 1922.

31 DMC, 16 July 1922; 5 Aug. 1922.

32 DMC, 7 July 1922; 31 July 1922.

33 DMC, 6 July 1922; 15 July 1922.

34 DMC, 16 July 1922; 7 July 1922; 15 July 1922.

35 DMC, 22 July 1922; 26 July 1922.

36 DMC, 2 July 1922. He noted the Four Courts again on 7 July 1922 and 'Return of mace (Four Courts)' on 12 July 1922.

37 DMC, 6 July 1922.

38 DMC, 3 Aug. 1922. The landings of soldiers at Kerry on 2 August had resulted in a number of casualties. He attended the funerals of nine soldiers killed in these landings on 8 August. Michael Collins to Kitty Kiernan, 4 Aug. 1922, Ó Broin (ed.), *In great haste*, 220.

39 Michael Collins to Kitty Kiernan, 8 Aug. 1922, Ó Broin (ed.), *In great haste*, 221.

40 Michael Collins to Kitty Kiernan, 8 Aug. 1922, Ó Broin (ed.), *In great haste*, 221.

'TAKING OVER GENERALLY'

1   DMC, 14 Oct. 1921; Seán Cromien, 'J.J. McElligott', *Dictionary of Irish biography*, https://www.dib.ie/biography/mcelligott-james-john-jimmy-a5654 [accessed 24 June 2022].

2   DMC, 7 June 1919; 29 Sept. 1920.

3   DMC, 12 Oct. 1921.

4   DMC, 13 Oct. 1921.

5   DMC, 16 Oct. 1921. McElligott came back to Dublin in 1923 and took the role of assistant secretary at the Department of Finance. Four years later he became secretary.

6   See Anna Devlin, 'Imagining Ireland's economic future in the early twentieth century', PhD thesis, TCD.

7   DMC, 15 Nov. 1919. John Chartres met Collins in 1918. He attended the Treaty negotiations as second secretary to the delegation. He attended the one meeting of the negotiations' committee on financial relations. See Richard Hawkins & Pauric J. Dempsey, 'John Smith Chartres', *Dictionary of Irish biography*, https://www.dib.ie/biography/chartres-john-smith-a1625 [accessed 24 June 2022].

8   DMC, 22 Feb. 1920.

9   DMC, 23 Feb. 1920.

10 DMC, 12 Jan. 1922; 13 Jan. 1922; 26 Jan. 1922. MacMahon may refer to James MacMahon, Under Secretary for Ireland, who oversaw the administrative handover. See Patrick Maume, 'James MacMahon', *Dictionary of Irish biography*, https://www.dib.ie/biography/macmahon-james-a5258 [accessed 24 June 2022].

11 DMC, 28 Jan. 1922.

12 DMC, 20 Feb. 1922.

13 DMC, 28 June 1922.

14 DMC, 31 Jan. 1922.

15 DMC, 20 Apr. 1922.

16 See Patrick Long, 'Diarmuid Fawsitt', *Dictionary of Irish biography*, https://www.dib.ie/biography/fawsitt-diarmuid-jeremiah-a3024 [accessed 24 June 2022].

17 DMC, 9 Mar. 1922; See Eda Sagarra, *Kevin O'Shiel: Tyrone nationalist and Irish state-builder* (Dublin, 2013).

18 DMC, 20 Apr. 1922. See also 21 Mar. 1922, 23 Mar. 1922, 31 Mar. 1922, 11 Apr. 1922, 20 Apr. 1922, 22 May 1922, 24 May 1922.

19 'Report of sub-committee on land purchase', *Report of the proceedings of the Irish convention* (Dublin, 1918).

20 DMC, 2 Aug. 1922; 24 Apr. 1922; 12 May 1922.

21 DMC, 15 July 1922; 20 July 1922.

22 DMC, 17 May 1922.

23 DMC, 5 July 1922; 10 Apr. 1922; 18 Jan. 1922; 1 Apr. 1922; 27 Mar. 1922; Michael Collins to Desmond Fitzgerald, 12 July 1922 (NAI, TSCH/3/S595).

24 DMC, 28 Jan. 1922; Michael Collins to Desmond Fitzgerald, 12 July 1922 (NAI, TSCH/3/S595).

25 Michael Collins to Desmond Fitzgerald, 12 July 1922 (NAI, TSCH/3/S595). Northcliffe was Alfred Harmsworth, owner of the *Daily Mail* and the *Daily Mirror*.

26 DMC, 25 Jan. 1922; 18 Jan. 1922; 19 Jan. 1922; 20 Jan. 1922.

27 DMC, 26 Jan. 1922; Diarmaid Ferriter, 'Sir Joseph Glynn', *Dictionary of Irish biography*, https://www.dib.ie/biography/glynn-sir-joseph-a3499 [accessed 24 June 2022].

28 DMC, 18 July 1922; 27 Apr. 1922.

29 DMC, 1 Mar. 1922. Application for a service certificate by John Crowley, 28 Dec. 1935 (MSPC, MSP34REF38741).

30 DMC, 20 Mar. 1922; 22 Apr. 1922. McCarthy was a publican and had been boycotted by the IRA for serving crown forces. McCarthy's premises were fired into in the early hours of 27 April 1922, the first of three nights of violence in the Bandon valley, that resulted in the deaths of ten people. McCarthy may or may not have been a target that night. See Peter Hart, *The IRA and its enemies: violence and community in Cork, 1916–1923* (Oxford, 1998), 274; Andy Bielenberg, John Borgonovo, James S. Donnelly Jr, '"Something in the nature of a massacre": the Bandon valley killings revisited', *Éire-Ireland*, 9, 3&4 (Fall/Winter, 2014), 22.

31 DMC, 15 June 1922.

32 DMC, 24 Apr. 1922; 3 May 1922; 9 May 1922; 11 May 1922.

33 DMC, 17 Jan. 1922.

34 DMC, 24 July 1922.

35 DMC, 19 Mar. 1922; 24 Mar. 1922; 18 Apr. 1922; 16 May 1922.

36 Michael Collins to Kitty Kiernan, 16 Jan. 1922, Ó Broin (ed.), *In great haste*, 105.

ACKNOWLEDGEMENTS

From the authors

We incurred a number of debts of gratitude in the course of writing this book. Special thanks to the National Archives of Ireland, and most especially to Orlaith McBride, Zoë Reid, Karen Downey and Elizabeth McEvoy. Dave Garavin, Declan Behan, Diarmuid Slattery and all at New Graphic have turned an idea about how to tackle Collins's diaries into a beautiful book—many thanks. Equally, to Ruth Hegarty and Liz Evers of the Royal Irish Academy our heartfelt thanks.

A book as richly illustrated as this one is a testament to the resources of a wide range of libraries, archives, and museums and to the expertise of their librarians, archivists and curators. In particular, we would like to thank the National Library of Ireland, and most especially Katherine McSharry. Thanks also to the Military Archives, the National Museum of Ireland, Kilmainham Gaol Museum, the Michael Collins House Museum, Clonakilty, UCD Archives, The National Archives, London, Oireachtas Library, RTÉ Archives, GAA Museum, Waterford County Museum, Dungarvan, Library of Congress and British Pathé. Thanks to David Meehan and Gordon Kennedy at Special Collections and Archives, DCU Library. To Albert Fenton, a special note of appreciation for the kind permission to reproduce a letter to him from Emmet Dalton.

This is a better book for the insights of Mark Duncan and Ciarán Wallace. Any mistakes, of course, are our own. Thanks to our colleagues at Dublin City University and Trinity College Dublin.

Finally, special thanks to Catherine Cox and Joseph Clarke.

From the National Archives and Royal Irish Academy'

The National Archives and Royal Irish Academy would like to thank the family of the late Liam and Betty Collins, Clonakilty, County Cork for their generous loan of the diaries to the National Archives. *Days in the life: reading the Michael Collins diaries, 1918–1922* is published in the context of the National Archives' 2022 Commemoration Programme as part of the Decade of Centenaries 2012–2023.